Working the Territory

Working the Territory

60 Years of Advertising
from the People of
Needham Harper Worldwide

Paul Harper

Prentice-Hall, Inc.
Englewood Cliffs, New Jersey

Prentice-Hall International, Inc., *London*
Prentice-Hall of Australia, Pty. Ltd., *Sydney*
Prentice-Hall Canada, Inc., *Toronto*
Prentice-Hall of India Private Ltd., *New Delhi*
Prentice-Hall of Japan, Inc., *Tokyo*
Prentice-Hall of Southeast Asia Pte. Ltd., *Singapore*
Whitehall Books, Ltd., *Wellington, New Zealand*
Editora Prentice-Hall do Brasil Ltda., *Rio de Janeiro*
Prentice-Hall Hispanoamericana, S.A., *Mexico*

Library of Congress Cataloging-in-Publication Data

Harper, Paul
  Working the territory.

   1. Needham Harper Worldwide—History.
2. Advertising agencies—United States—History.
3. Advertising campaigns—History.   I. Title.
HF6181.N44H37 1985   338.7′616591′0973   85-19096

ISBN 0-13-967563-9

Printed in the United States of America

This book is dedicated to all the people who created its contents over the past sixty years, and who seem to share those qualities that make great advertising people:

Common sense,
Intuition,
Flair,
and Courage.

Paul Harper
May, 1985

ACKNOWLEDGMENTS

This is to gratefully acknowledge the help of Danielle Wierengo in assembling the material and helping me in a variety of editorial functions. She was ably assisted by Virginia Selden. Amy Burns and Jodi Elovich were of invaluable assistance in locating and gathering the graphics. The production expertise of Carmine Marino, Richard Weber, and Bill Troy is reflected throughout as is the design skill of Steve Singer.

CONTENTS

Working the Territory

WORKING THE TERRITORY

I went to work at Needham, Louis and Brorby, a Chicago advertising agency, in 1946. I am still working there, although the name has changed to Needham Harper Worldwide, and I am in the enviable role of Chairman Emeritus. This role is enviable because people still smile at me, even though my work habits have become somewhat erratic.

It was not always so. In 1946, my first assignment as a junior copywriter was on Swift & Company's Animal Feeds. I was told to bone up on livestock nutrition, and then write advertisements for publications like the *Prairie Farmer* and *Hoard's Dairyman*. It was too much. Nothing in my Yale education, tempered by three years in the Marine Corps, had prepared me for this. My copy came back with blue scrawls on it saying, "Speak English!" or "Who do you think you're talking to!" Finally, my boss called me in. He had a perplexed look on his face. "The only answer for you, Harper," he said, "is to get out and work the territory. Get out where the feed is fed. Ask questions and listen hard."

Two days later I was leaning on the gate of a farm in central Illinois. The farmer was feeding 300 cattle and 150 hogs for market. He bought lots of feed, none of it Swift's. "Got nothing against Swift's," he said. "It's just that the other fella talks my language."

I showed him a proposed ad. "What's this stuff about the romance of feeding?" he asked. "You think feeding is romantic, just step into that barn over there." I did so and got a noseful of dust and ammonia fumes. "All I want to know from you folks is how I'm going to get those steers ready for market a week sooner," he said.

Two weeks and 35 farms later, I was back at my desk in Chicago with a new picture of my reader. My pastoral ideal was shattered. I now knew that I was addressing a man who had to balance a half-dozen variables including the weather, just to squeeze out a small profit on his steers and hogs. My copy could help him manage one of those variables *if* I could get him to read it. I wasn't dealing in romance, I was dealing in raw, feed-lot economics.

My boss looked at the resulting copy. "You travel well," he said. I found this reassuring.

After that, "working the territory" became a habit of mind with me. I found that with every new assignment there was a new set of needs and attitudes to learn; sometimes even a new set of words. The sights, sounds, and smells of each part of the marketplace were different. The only way to write convincing advertising was to learn these things firsthand; to "get out and work the territory, get out where the feed is fed; ask questions and listen hard."

This, I found, was what gave the advertising business its hard, pragmatic flavor. It was also what gave it its color, motion, and endless variety.

This 1947 advertisement for hog feed shows the results of the author's visits to feed lots throughout the Corn Belt.

THE VALUE OF HISTORY

A few months ago I sat down to write a history of our advertising agency. We were going strong after 60 years in business. A fine new management team had just been installed, and my partners and I thought it would be useful to record some of the things we had learned.

I explained my project to a well-known scholar. "Not so!" he proclaimed. "An advertising agency, by definition, has no history."

"An agency's products," he went on to say, "are highly perishable ideas and images. It deals entirely in the present and the future, so its past is irrelevant, except to curio hounds and anesthetists."

I was worried. If what he said was true, my peers and I and our work would soon become mere shards in the dustbins of the marketplace.

I decided to write this history anyway.

Of course, an advertising agency has to move with the culture; preferably ahead of it. There is certainly no room in an agency for icons or busted couches.

Any effective organization has a core of values that are expressed in its work, and in the morale of its people. Those values evolve over time. They generally bear the mark of a succession of management personalities. Their power is *cumulative* and they are what drives an organization forward.

These values shouldn't have to be reexamined in every crisis, or reinvented every fiscal year. They are, in fact, best understood through an agency's history.

Maurice Needham had founded our agency back in the Coolidge era, an act which, in itself, set a standard for courage. For over thirty-five years, he and his partners, Mel Brorby and Jack Louis, labored to establish a reputation for honest, effective work, and a deep concern for people.

The same kind of thing could be said about my own partners. Jim Isham, Blair Vedder, and Keith Reinhard are just as committed to the idea that a creative organization will run best if it has a collective sense of pride, principle, and mutual respect. Without this sense, we agree, we would be left with nothing but a power structure and a bank account; interesting, but not good enough for the long pull.

There have been many challenges to these rather simple values over the years, both from within and without. There were the rascals and mountebanks; but mainly there was the trouble caused by perfectly

4

natural lapses of confidence or will. In a business such as ours, with its frequent clashes of judgment, one has to have resilience, which is rooted in confidence, which, in turn, is rooted in a knowledge of what has come before. Again, there is a place for history.

The real hallmark of an advertising agency is how well it can deal with the turbulence of the marketplace. That can be like trying to stake out turf in the Arctic Ocean during the spring thaw. There are ways to help clients not only define turf, but to start things, "grow them," defend them, change strategies, and "grow them" again.

These things can be learned; not through heavy, chronological histories, but by occasional reminders about what worked, and why, and what has changed over time, and what has not. That is what this book is about.

Getting Going

The tradesman, venturing into a new town, must be strong of heart and of good disposition. For he must please the magistrates, pay his debts, and make himself widely and well known to the people.

Rules of Commerce
Paris, 1760

8

MAURICE NEEDHAM

In 1925, in Chicago, Maurice Needham began work as owner and operator of his own advertising agency. He had four clients and just enough revenue to pay the bills and make a small profit. Among his formidable competitors across town were Jim Young and Henry Stanton of J. Walter Thompson, and Albert Lasker and Claude Hopkins of Lord and Thomas (later Foote Cone and Belding). When Maurice retired thirty-seven years later, he and his partners had built an agency that could compete with them on any basis except sheer size.

As this record suggests, he knew the values of consistency and steadfastness. The advertising business was changing rapidly from one of simple, more or less personal, exchanges, to one of sophisticated creative modes and elaborate selling structures. Maurice saw all along, that "There is really no advertising problem that cannot be solved by bright people if they trust one another and are daring and tough."

To Maurice, trust was what held a business together, and daring was what made it grow. Toughness was not an empty posture; it was what gave a business resilience and earned it respect. This point of view made the agency an exciting place to work. Although the perils of our business were always there, we had a sense that none of us would ever suffer undeserved defeat.

Maurice was a man of great personal dignity, combined with a sincere common touch. His reserve was the mark of great determination; but it never concealed for long a deep interest in each of us, great and small.

His wife, Ray, supervised the design and decoration of the offices as the agency expanded. Her insights into the business, as well as her good taste, were of benefit to all of us.

For Maurice, the inner man was fed by deep and reciprocated loyalty between him and those he admired, inside the business and out. It was also fed by a deep knowledge of things as diverse as poetry and war. Among his friends were Carl Sandburg, the poet, George Halas, owner of the Chicago Bears, Adlai Stevenson, the statesman, and David Ogilvy, a very talented competitor.

Maurice was really a family man, and those of us who worked for him felt like part of an extended family, scrappy and contentious, but happy at our work.

World-wide Banking Service

Through more than fifty years of constant growth and thousands of direct business connections established both here and abroad, the Illinois Merchants Trust Company has built a service for importers, exporters, banks, travelers, and investors, which is truly world-wide in character.

The resources of this bank are large; its organization is well developed; its facilities highly specialized and its board of directors composed of leaders in every branch of commerce and industry.

Inquiries about our services and our ability to meet your banking needs are cordially invited.

ILLINOIS MERCHANTS TRUST COMPANY

Capital & Surplus 45 *Million Dollars*

LA SALLE JACKSON, CLARK AND QUINCY STREETS · CHICAGO

Advertisements for two of the agency's original accounts.

10

Paint White
or light colors

EAGLE
Pure WHITE LEAD
OLD DUTCH PROCESS

MELVIN BRORBY

Melvin Brorby was Maurice Needham's first partner. On the day the new agency opened, he was designated as "the writer," which meant that he was the creative director. Mel brought an extraordinary background to this job; his early career began in a small town in Iowa, and extended to Oxford and the Sorbonne, to a residency in India, and then home to the advertising business.

It is said that the test of a truly literate person is the ability to make plain people understand complicated matters. Mel brought to his work not only penetrating thought, but clear and colorful language. In an era when the printed page was the central medium, this served the agency well.

In 1930, the agency won its first major award, The Harvard Award for Advertising Excellence, for his work, a powerful piece of copy for the investment house of A. G. Becker. As the agency moved into the broadcast era, he put his talents to work on the strategy and language of the new media, establishing standards of warmth and humanity that became a hallmark of the agency's advertising.

Mel's many interests brought the agency into contact with a wide range of professional and intellectual resources. He was a founding Chairman of the Chicago Council on Foreign Relations, Chairman of the American Association of Advertising Agencies, and later, Chairman of the Wingspread Foundation, a cultural forum founded by the Johnson family in Racine, Wisconsin. Mel taught us that the world of advertising really has no limits and that experience and knowledge of all kinds can give us a better grasp of our profession. He showed us all the importance of being part of the wider world.

M A R K E T S   O N   T H E   M A R C H .

- They march along—out of one market into another. Children growing up, marrying, making new homes. Men and women passing into old age, leaving behind the varied needs of active life.
- The markets of business are never fixed. Today's market is today's possession only. Tomorrow's army of buyers is but now massing forward—largely unaware of the products and services industry offers them.
- In this endless procession there is the key to every manufacturer's sales problem and a challenge to his resourcefulness. His success in gaining and holding these changing markets is measured by his knowledge of them, and by his ability to supply what people want at the time they want it.
- The alertness of a company's management in meeting this problem is of prime importance to the investor. Plants and inventories lose their value quickly if markets disappear. Earnings diminish when management fails to maintain that constant flow of new customers which replaces those lost, in the natural order of things, each year.
- Since its inception, 37 years ago, A. G. Becker & Co. has been particularly concerned with the management factor. Long before detailed financial statements were available, this company was financing American industry in large measure on the basis of its appraisal of management. And today, our estimate of management is still the determining factor in our recommendation of securities.
- The nature of the comprehensive investment service built up on this basis is described in a booklet, copy of which will be sent you upon request. Ask for T108.

BONDS · STOCKS · COMMERCIAL PAPER · 54 PINE STREET, NEW YORK · 100 SOUTH LA SALLE STREET, CHICAGO

A. G. Becker & Co.

Winner of one of the 1930 Harvard Awards for Outstanding Advertising.

14

—The Original
"One-man"
PORTABLE
Radio

Weighs only 24 pounds

1 The first high-grade radio receiver that's *really portable.* Easy to carry. Small enough to slip under a Pullman seat.

All in one small case

2 Batteries, loud speaker, loop aerial, 5 tubes. No ground connections. No aerial to be strung up. No electric socket connections.

Retails for **$84²⁵** *complete*

3 $65.00 without accessories. Sweet tone. Strong volume. Distance. Selectivity. Under rigid tests, actually out-performs many big sets. Standard parts.

Trav-ler

Advertisement for Trav-ler, the first portable radio.

JOHN LOUIS

In 1929, John Louis joined Maurice and Mel, and the agency became Needham, Louis and Brorby. Jack had an extraordinary combination of charm and keen business sense. He had an incisive mind, but he spoke with discretion, economy, and humor. He never brushed anyone aside. As a result, he was always listened to; his judgments were eagerly awaited.

He was the perfect man to take the agency into broadcasting and show business. His own interests led him in this direction, and he did so with quiet aggressiveness and good taste. From a rather modest start with "Russell Pratt's Topsy Turvy Time," Jack Louis rapidly

Babe Ruth and Lou Gehrig at Cub's Park in 1929, where the agency pioneered the use of major league baseball commercially for the Trav-Ler Radio Company and other clients.

17

expanded the agency's radio billings with such national leaders as "Fibber McGee and Molly" for Johnson's Wax, and "The Great Gildersleeve" for Kraft.

He then guided the agency into the television era with the same skill, using drama, as in "Robert Montgomery Presents" and personality shows with such people as Garry Moore and Steve Allen.

As a result of Jack's orchestration, the agency's presence and reputation in the broadcast industry far exceeded its billings. In an era when agencies had far more to do with program standards than they have at present, Jack's high standards had wide effects. He understood popular tastes, but he would not compromise on quality.

To those of us in the vineyards, however, it was Jack's cool, unerring advertising judgment and his friendly support that were the mark of the man.

In 1940, the agency received the Annual Advertising Award for Outstanding Radio Production for its work on "Fibber McGee and Molly." The leading trade magazine, Advertising and Selling, *was the donor.*

Setting Standards

Advertising is neither an art nor a science, although it borrows from both. It is a blending of persuasive effects, some new, some old, that together, build a vivid and appealing product personality.

SETTING STANDARDS

In the year 1590, an innkeeper, seeking to attract visitors to the Leipzig Fair, hung out a sign saying:

Sleep Well.
Dry Straw.
No Rats.

This early advertiser knew what the tired traveler wanted: comfort, safety, and rest; and he offered these things simply and clearly.

On the Aegean island of Kos are the ruins of an ancient Greek health resort. On a worn and chipped block of marble are carved the words:

Well-being is the gift of the Gods.

The manager of this spa knew what a sick Greek wanted. He knew that he couldn't promise it outright, so he was really saying "Relax and have faith in the process."

Very little has changed in the intervening centuries. The underlying principles of good advertising are the same. Tastes change. Language changes. Products, markets, and media change. Underneath it all, people don't change.

The strengths and frailties of human nature are always with us. The needs for self-respect, love, security, accomplishment, and power are never ending. Tides of fashion come and go, and they will affect the way we tell our story. Beneath the technique, there has to be an appeal to man, woman, or child that rings a primal bell.

Today, the competition for attention is so great that the source of attention is often forgotten. The source of attention is not a "target audience," and it is not a circulation base. It is a needy, prideful, skeptical, sometimes gullible, but, in the end, practical human being.

The biggest mistakes in advertising are made when:

* novelty replaces insight;
* noise displaces empathy;
* technical fireworks replace humanity.

The most effective innovations in advertising are those which:

* surprise without shock;
* please without puffery;
* inform without boring.

Past experience confirms all this. We can learn from the cumulative experience of our profession, which goes back a long time.

It does no good to set down narrow rules for creating advertising. Rules are for people who don't really understand what they are doing, and have to be led by the hand. Rules contradict the idea that in the advertising business we are dealing with the unpredictable, fickle, and fascinating human race. The creators of advertising need plenty of psychological turf; so, instead of rules, our agency has set down a few general guidelines for the creation of advertising. The reader will notice that they focus on the individual prospect. This is still, after all, a person-to-person business.

It is a matter of principle with our agency that these guidelines be followed. They are broad enough to accommodate any thoughtful form of person-to-person communication.

---

1. ESTABLISH A PRODUCT PERSONALITY

Effective advertising invests the product with a vivid, appealing personality that helps it stand out from the crowd. Like a friendly face, it signals genuine values, in likable ways.

Building product personality takes *consistency.* Advertising, packaging, promotion, product design, must all speak with the same voice. Building product personality takes *time* as well. Awareness can be achieved overnight. Familiarity and acceptance take longer; but once created, this personality can be the most valuable and enduring asset a product has.

▶

This award-winning commercial for State Farm insurance helped personalize the world's largest insurer of autos. The egg symbolized the vulnerability of car and driver. The giant helping hand symbolized the caring and attentive service State Farm offers. A clear-cut product personality emerges.

1

Handle with care.

2

That's what this familiar emblem really says. And you'll get one like it when you insure your car with State Farm—the biggest car insurance company there is.

3

Then wherever you drive, whether your need for claim service is large or small,

4

you'll have a friend nearby to handle everything with care.

5

See your local State Farm Mutual agent soon and have your car marked for careful handling. You'll be surprised at how little it costs; probably less than you're shelling out now.

6

Theme: "And like a good neighbor, State Farm is there."

2. POSITION THE PRODUCT CLEARLY

Effective advertising makes it instantly clear where the product fits into the prospect's life. Is it competing on its style or its utility? Is it a health product or a beauty product? Is its value in its quality or its economy? Clear positioning picks the arena in which the product is most likely to succeed. It lets the prospect focus quickly on whatever specific benefit is being offered.

ake it simple.

This billboard helped position Honda with absolute clarity in its category. It projects both the simplicity and class that is the hallmark of the product and its marketing efforts.

3. FEATURE THE MOST COMPELLING BENEFIT

Effective advertising addresses a real need. It speaks as competitively as the facts and good taste allow. It is specific and single-minded. It may use imagery, but it never shrouds the product and its benefit in technique. The product, not the advertising, emerges as the star.

opy small, nd large.

The best thing about the Xerox 3100 LDC isn't that it makes incredibly clear, sharp copies. Or that it's portable. Or that it can copy light originals, bulky bound volumes, or even photographs.

It's not even that it has easy-to-load paper cassettes and a document feeder.

It's the fact that it can make size-for-size copies from documents as small as 8½ x 11 to as large as 14 x 18. And any size in between.

So now you can copy letters, ledger sheets, even oversize computer printout, all with one machine.

The Xerox 3100 Large Document Copier. Because one size doesn't fit all.

XEROX

14 x 18

To the buyer of copying machines, an important new benefit is made instantly clear.

4. BREAK THE PATTERN

Effective advertising excites the ear and eye with a look and sound of its own. It separates itself from surrounding communications, just as it separates the product from competing products. But it pulls this excitement from the product itself, in ways that reflect the character of the product.

Borrowed interest is never as effective as intrinsic interest.

The purpose of this advertising is to establish that there is now a light beer called Bud Light—and that it is worth asking for by name. The spectacular plays on the word "light" break the pattern of beer advertising—and of light beer advertising in particular.

1

Don't just ask for a light beer.

2

"Gimme a light."

3

Ask them to bring out their best.
"Bud Light?"
Bud Light.

4

Because everything else is just a light.

1

Don't just ask for a light beer.

2

"Gimme a light."

3

Ask them to bring out their best.
"Bud Light?"
Bud Light.

4

Because everything else is just a light.

5. GENERATE TRUST

A prospect will not buy from a salesman he does not trust. Effective advertising, therefore, not only speaks the truth, everything about it rings true. Even when fantasy is used, it is a fantasy which the viewer can share, accept, and find motivating.

It is simple, direct, empathic.

There is no such thing as a "common" cold.

NO two people are alike.

And no two colds are alike.

For example, what may be a simple runny nose for you could be a real problem for someone else.

Not only that, you can

So how do you know what to take?

Well, some cold medicine manufacturers think you and your family should take one powerful cold medicine to relieve more symptoms than you may actually have.

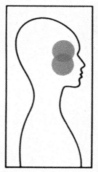
Triaminic® Syrup
Stuffy nose
Runny nose

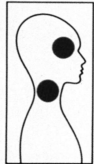
Triaminic-DM®
Stuffy nose
Frequent cough

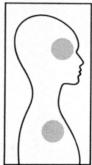
Triaminic® Expectorant
Stuffy nose
Dry, hacking cough

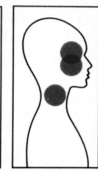
Triaminicol® Syrup
Stuffy nose, Runny nose
Frequent cough

have a dry, hacking cough with a runny or stuffy nose.

Or a dry, hacking cough without a runny nose.

Or any other number of combinations.

© 1983 Dorsey Laboratories, Division of Sandoz, Inc.
Use only as directed.

We don't.

Because we don't want you to be overmedicated.

After all, when all you have is a stuffy nose, why take products with a cough

ppressant or fever reducer?
nd if you're dealing with a
ugh, why risk possible
mach upset with a prod-
that contains aspirin?

WHICH is why
Triaminic®
makes four
different cold
dicines. For four different
ges and combinations of
nptoms of a cold. They all
ntain a decongestant to
ckly clear nasal passages.
cause one thing you
pect from cold medicines
 let you breathe freer, fast.
    But none of them
ntain aspirin. Because we
l aspirin or other pain
evers are something you
uld only take when the
nptoms require it.
    Each Triaminic formula
ats specific symptoms,
h in its own unique way.
    Triaminic® Syrup is for
 stuffy, runny nose of
old.
    Triaminic-DM® Cough
rmula effectively relieves
annoying, persistent

cough and nasal congestion.
    To break up congestion
when you have a dry,
hacking cough, we make
Triaminic® Expectorant.
    And Triaminicol® a
multi-symptom cold syrup,
is designed especially for
three specific symptoms:
nasal congestion, frequent
coughing and runny nose.
    And they're all safe and
effective, so they've been
recommended by physicians
and pharmacists for years.

SO, the next time you
get the so-called
"common" cold, try
Triaminic.
    We won't treat your
cold in a common way. ₂₇₈₂₃

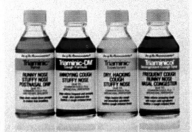

Triaminic

Why take more than you need.

This campaign for Dorsey's Triaminic cough and cold syrups recognizes customer confusion over the array of new cold products and their claims. Taking the customer's side, it sorts out what Dorsey has to offer in a way that wins trust and understanding.

6. APPEAL TO BOTH HEART AND HEAD

No sale is made entirely in the mind. All sales are made at least partly in the heart. Effective advertising, therefore, does more than present practical reasons to buy. It invests the message with real emotional values consistent with the product's personality.

"I made it myself"

    To a child these words are among the happiest in the English language.
    Not too many toys encourage children to say them.
    Ours can.
    In fact, without imagination our toys would never run.
    And we wouldn't want it any other way.
    Give your child a Crayola® gift like the Crayon Carrousel or Draw N' Do Desk and you can watch creativity in progress. An eager young mind at work.
    And does it really matter that there's no such thing as a green chicken?
    Or that Uncle Fred looks like he doesn't have ears?
    What matters is that it's something from the imagination.
    And something from the heart.
    We can't think of a better toy than that.

Our toys run on imagination.

This advertising for Crayola reasons with the parents of young children. At the same time it offers a deep and important emotional reward to both parent and child. It appeals to both heart and head.

Some Cases in Point

The ideas, campaigns, and programs on the following pages are the work of many people. They worked in groups, pairs, and more often than not as individuals, putting facts, images, and intuitions together until things became magically clear—and the outlines of a product personality emerged.

Their success was based on knowledge of the people they were trying to persuade. This knowledge was gained by learning the marketplace firsthand—by *working the territory.*

These cases were selected to represent the broadest spectrum of creative problems, and to illustrate, thereby, the usefulness of the agency's guidelines in any situation.

Since the selection was limited to this purpose, not all our clients are represented. The wealth of good work of our international partners, which could not possibly have been treated fairly in this context, has also had to be omitted.

WHEN THE MEDIUM REALLY WAS THE MESSAGE

Fibber McGee and Molly and the Rise of Johnson's Wax

There was a time of innocence in American advertising when people could sit back, turn on the radio, and listen to friendly, familiar voices that made them chuckle and relax. Hour after hour, they could create their own visual images because there wasn't anything to watch. Program blended into commercial and back into program again. There were few harsh intrusions into this land of fantasy. The products advertised in this disarming atmosphere often became part of the show and came to enjoy the same acceptance as the program. In effect they borrowed personality from the show.

Johnny Florea, LIFE *Magazine, © Time Inc.*

Harlow Wilcox and Fibber McGee and Molly greet the audience at the NBC Studio.

Through our agency, Johnson's Wax sponsored the weekly half-hour radio comedy, "Fibber McGee and Molly" from 1935 until 1950. It was one of the longest sponsorships in broadcast history. During that time, under the insightful leadership of its chairman, H. F. Johnson, the company became synonymous with floor and furniture care. Brands such as Glo-Coat became the undisputed leaders in their fields, and a succession of new household products was launched.

Seldom has the rise of a major marketer been linked so closely to a single commercial vehicle. Almost never has there been such a sustained and sympathetic relationship between a show of any kind and an audience.

The character, Fibber McGee, was Mr. Everyman, canny but blundering, tolerant but suspicious, willful and bluff, and easily checked by his wife, Molly.

Molly was kitchen-smart. She could see through all kinds of humbug. She stood ready to let the air out of Fibber's tires when they became overinflated, and was equally willing to pump them up again. Together they represented the comic side of marriage as it was seen in those days.

They treated Harlow Wilcox, the announcer, with a kind of friendly skepticism that never failed to set him up for a disarming pitch. By kidding Wilcox's commercials, Fibber and Molly made them irresistible. Some of the commercials were straightforward, others were ingeniously woven into the script. All of them shared the earthy, down-home quality that made the show itself so appealing.

The combined effect of program and commercials was warm without being sticky, and funny without being barbaric. It was peopled with characters, not cartoons. Behind the pratfalls and insults were real people, whose dignity remained intact.

All those qualities established not only brand personalities for Johnson's products, they established a corporate personality for Johnson, which helped its dynamic growth.

The show provided a selling environment that cannot be duplicated today. The challenge is to reproduce some of the values it represented in the current environment.

Like many advertisers during World War II, Johnson's Wax shifted much of its reduced marketing budget to public service advertising. Molly McGee urged women to take war jobs, thus releasing men for the armed forces.

Introducing Swift's Meats for Babies

In 1947, the agency's first major new product introduction after the war brought forth Swift's Meats for Babies. This introduction successfully hurdled prejudice against feeding meat to infants and the prevailing lack of knowledge about proteins.

A TRIUMPH OF BRAND PERSONALITY

Morton Salt

About 1914, someone who knew what he or she was doing, designed a label for Morton Salt. It had a trademark and a slogan that are still in use today. Morton salt was free-flowing, which helped in sticky weather. What better way of expressing this, than *"When it rains, it pours."* Over the years, a series of people who knew what they were doing left the trademark and the slogan pretty much alone.

When our agency got the Morton account in 1947, the blue and yellow label was already among the half-dozen most widely recognized in the food store. Although table salt was certainly among the least

intriguing of products, our predecessors had managed to create a classic brand personality. Our job was clearly to keep this personality alive, current, and highly visible.

There wasn't much you could say about salt, but we were helped by Morton's merchandising policy, which was to tie salt displays in with seasonal foods. This gave us creative latitude of which we took full advantage.

The merchandising and the advertising worked together to keep Morton dominant in its category—and to give the brand a far greater share of mind than its intrinsic interest warranted. Morton Salt is a classic example of building and maintaining product personality against the odds. The keys were consistency in strategy, variety in execution, and willingness to say very little when there was very little to say.

Billboards linked to store displays.

When it rains it pours....

America's best selling table salt More people use Morton's because
"when it rains it pours" Available plain or iodized
(Morton pioneered iodized salt 29 years ago to help prevent simple goiter)

Iodized
or Plain

Morton's campaign in LIFE *Magazine.*

MEANWHILE, DOWN ON THE FARM ...

Massey-Ferguson Humanizes Farm Machinery Advertising

To many advertisers, hardware is hardware, to be presented as a useful accumulation of bolts, pistons, wheels, and extrusions covered with a distinctive paint job. In the 1950s, much farm machinery advertising had just this quality—the quality of a thorough and detailed salesman's spec sheet (to be read with special lenses).

To break into this bustling market, Massey-Ferguson knew it had to do things differently. Its fine engineering had made it a world leader outside the United States. It had an exclusive feature, the Ferguson Hitch, which made it much easier to attach implements to a tractor, and to control them in the field. However, this advertiser was wise enough to know that it would take more than a mechanical feature to win the farmer's attention away from established giants such as International Harvester and John Deere. It needed to build a distinctive brand personality.

In 1957, we were given the job of developing that personality. Research and field work told us that, apart from use values, farmers took real pride in owning advanced, well-made equipment. Getting a brand new tractor or combine was not a routine event; it was the subject of much talk, and great interest. This was particularly true on the family farm, which was then still the backbone of American agriculture.

The result was *"the Massey-Ferguson Man,"* who was presented in the advertising as a tough minded, hardworking, and prideful individualist, an accurate reflection of any farmer who would buy a new and relatively unknown brand. The advertising used situations involving his family and neighbors. While not overdoing it, it appealed directly to the farmer's pride of ownership and gave him reasons for indulging his pride.

An anthem was composed called *"The Massey-Ferguson Kind of Man,"* which brought sales meetings to their feet, and won wide acclaim on radio.

As with many major purchases, advertising could only set the tone and present key facts about farm machinery. In making the sale, distribution was paramount; but the advertising did give Massey-Ferguson a platform of personality to stand on, from which to challenge the industry leaders.

It stands as an example of the importance of humanity in advertising, in fields which, at first glance, lend themselves only to cold presentation of fact.

44

modern farming's NEW pace-setter

LOOK DAD IT'S HERE!

The first big 4-plow tractor with the Ferguson System!

It had just been delivered to Massey-Ferguson dealer Bill Bailey's place . . . the completely new tractor that folks from miles around had been waiting to see: the power-packed all-new Massey-Ferguson 65.

They'd heard about it, and it had sounded mighty good. Why? It had the kind of power they wanted . . . ample power to work a 4-bottom plow under almost any conditions. But, most important, *it had the Ferguson Hydraulic System . . . the original tractor hydraulic system* and still engineered years ahead of all the rest. That's what made the MF-65 unique and exciting. It was the *first* tractor in the 4-plow power class with the Ferguson System and exclusive 4-way work control.

That's what brought the crowd to Massey-Ferguson dealer Bill Bailey's place of business that Saturday afternoon. They wanted to *see* the new MF-65 . . . get its big powerful feel. What they saw they liked. For what they saw and did, turn the page.

This message from Massey-Harris-Ferguson continues on next page

---

Look, compare . . . you'll be a Massey-Ferguson man!

GRASSLAND "MINUTE MEN"

They'll be tons ahead before others even get started!

When the dew is off the fields and the hay is right for working, Bob Miller rallies his crew with a hearty "Come on, boys, let's go!" And they're up and away without a minute wasted.

They hitch up their new fully mounted Massey-Ferguson 31 Dyna-Balance Mower in one minute flat. And there's no messy, time-consuming greasing to get their baler into action. It's the famous Massey-Ferguson No. 3 Baler . . . the one and only baler that's completely self-lubricated, with factory-sealed bearings throughout!

There's not a grease fitting anywhere on the Massey-Ferguson No. 3 Baler; it's always ready to go. With its 10-tons-an-hour capacity, it's out in the field and tons ahead before the others even get started!

Important too is the kind of bales the Massey-Ferguson No. 3 delivers with its exclusive Leaf-Guard design. Profit-making bales, with more of the protein-rich leaves saved. Uniform, perfectly tied bales, bale after bale, that stand up to roughest handling.

It's this kind of grassland performance that makes Bob Miller a Massey-Ferguson man!

One minute, and he's ready to mow! The fast hitch on the new fully mounted MF 31 Mower takes just a minute or two. From then on, it's fast, easy going under any field conditions. The Dyna-Balance Drive eliminates noisy, wearing vibration. And just a simple adjustment of the exclusive Variable Speed Belt Pulley regulates knife speed without additional pulleys or belts!

Exclusive 6-bar reel design saves more leaves . . . insures fast, clean raking with a slower reel speed for gentler handling, less leaf shattering. And the Massey-Ferguson Side-Delivery Rake actually moves the hay 50% less distance from swath to windrow for additional protection against shattering. Fully mounted with PTO drive . . . also available in pull-type model.

New MF 60 Flail-type Forage Harvester works for you the year 'round . . . does more jobs . . . everything from shredding tough, tangled stalks for mulch, to chopping tender green forage for feed. It even converts to a profitable hammer mill! First cost is low compared with other foragers that can't do nearly as much. Maintenance is low too . . . no auger, knife assembly, blower fan.

Now it's *MASSEY FERGUSON*

Massey-Ferguson Inc., Racine, Wisconsin
*Pace-Setter of Modern Farming . . .
World's Most Famous Combine and the
Only Tractors with the Ferguson System*

The Happy Marriage of Jack Benny and State Farm

During the '50s, as television became the family medium, it adopted the traditions of radio comedy. TV economics still made full or half-sponsorships possible on a weekly basis. TV could therefore offer an integrated framework that identified the product with the star and the ambiance of the show. For a few brief, bright years, some of the most effective advertising ever done resulted from the intimate relationship between the television program and the product. Instead of having to shout down or otherwise divert attention from the program, advertisers were still able to use the program to disarm the audience and amplify their message in many ways, on and off the air. The power of audience involvement and personal salesmanship was never clearer.

By 1960, State Farm had been the leading insurer of automobiles for eighteen years. It had reached this position by offering low-cost policies backed by good service; but the company had reached the great size at which its image needed warming up. Policyholders and prospects needed to be reassured that they were regarded as people, not as statistics. State Farm needed reselling on the most personal level. Agent training was stepped up in this direction; but the company needed a mass media spokesman.

At this point, the agency brought Jack Benny to State Farm. By 1960, Jack Benny had been a broadcast star for over 25 years. His concerns over his age (never over 39) and his money (did you ever see a man with shorter arms and lower pockets?) had gained the status of national house jokes.

A five-year cosponsorship followed which is one of the most effective sales relationships on record. Benny brought a low-interest proposition to life. His obsession with thrift fitted in with State Farm's low rates. He loved to work with the commercial writers. He loved to taunt Don Wilson, the good-natured and enthusiastic announcer. He threw himself into the long integrated commercials and made them a consummate blend of selling points and his brand of wry offhand humor. Once again program and product personality were merged and the product personality was greatly strengthened.

Benny's audience was big, it was loyal, and it responded. "The Jack Benny Show" was the spearhead of a total program that increased

Jack Benny and announcer Don Wilson play together in two of the program's many integrated commercials.

48

earned premiums on auto insurance for State Farm at half again the rate of the industry. State Farm's share of this enormous market grew from 10 percent to 12 percent, over the period of the sponsorship.

As with Fibber McGee and Molly, the structure of "The Jack Benny Show" is almost impossible to reproduce today. But its intangible values are a continuing reminder of the worth of personal salesmanship and a compatible advertising environment.

How HFC Changed the Image of the Small Loan Industry

The subject of money is freighted with more emotion than anything but sex. Most advertising for money services tends to run to extremes. It is either lofty and sanitary and handles the customer with rubber gloves, or it has a bargain basement flavor, getting as close to offering "easy money" as regulations will allow. The best money service advertising comes from companies who do not present themselves either as talking vaults on the one hand or as cash peddlers on the other, but who place themselves squarely in the customer's shoes and speak to his needs and anxieties.

In the 1950s, small loan offices still had the smell of the depression about them. They were located mostly on the second floors of run-down buildings. Borrowers entered furtively under a burden of guilt or desperation. Defaults were frequent.

The Household Finance Corporation, under its Chairman, H.F. McDonald, decided to change all that and go for a more prudent and reliable breed of borrower. HFC also sensed that underlying attitudes towards borrowing and debt were becoming rapidly more favorable. To address these changes, offices were moved down to the street level. The scary brass grilles were eliminated, and borrowers were now invited to sit down at desks opposite loan officers in natty red jackets.

The transformation of the loan office was complete. Now what was needed was advertising that spoke to the man or woman who needed money, but who still thought of borrowing as the last resort of the wastrel.

To address this cautious, agonizing person, a theme line was developed that was designed to put him or her at ease.

In 1956, on radio and television, HFC began telling people *"Never borrow money needlessly, but when you must, borrow from a company with folks you trust. Borrow confidently from HFC."*

The words were broadcast in the form of a rather soothing jingle. On TV the very simplest animation techniques were used to match the transmission difficulties of the time, and to project a straightforward yet genial image.

HFC's competitors reacted strongly, stating that HFC was telling people not to borrow and was therefore destroying the industry. Quite the opposite happened.

"Never borrow money needlessly" ran for seventeen years in various media. During that time, HFC's loan accounts increased over three times, making it clearly the industry leader. Its bad debt ratio went down because it was attracting a better grade of borrower. Its image changed from neutral to the industry's best. Its competitors, following HFC's lead, soon completed the transformation of this industry.

As with all service businesses, progress begins at the place of business. Advertising does no good if the service is not what is promised. HFC made good on its promises, but it was the advertising that put HFC clearly in the borrower's corner. It spoke directly to his fears and need for reassurance.

Today, financial service advertising has grown enormously in size, diversity, and sophistication. It is still those few advertisers who speak to the heart as well as the mind of the customer who win his lasting trust and loyalty.

51

1

You have a money problem, don't
you? Thought so. Know where you
may solve that problem with a loan?

2

Here, HFC (Household Finance)—
you want to know why HFC, don't
you? Well, oldest company since
1878, most experienced in solving
money problems. More than two
million people go there every
year—gives good advice too. Listen.

5

6

1956. The first
expression of a theme
that ran for 17 years.

3

4

7

8

Ken-L Ration's Answer to Dog Owners

In our work for Quaker's Ken-L Ration dog food (1952-1958), we found a unique kind of advertising response. Dog owners were no different from other people except when it came to their dogs. Plenty of affection was expected, both ways. When it came to feeding, however, a certain distancing took place. The person as dog owner was quite different from the person, say, as cake baker, glorying in the details of cake preparation. With the dog, the idea was to get a good meal into him with as little fuss as possible. The worst thing that could happen was to have the dog sniff the food and walk away, leaving the dog owner feeling silly and rejected.

Advertising, therefore, had to convince the dog owner; (1) that the dog would eat it; (2) that it was a full meal; (3) that it was easy to serve. The advertising could not be cold and perfunctory about this, because, after all, the dog owner did love the dog.

At the time we got the Ken-L Ration account, it was already the leading brand. It had gotten there with a superior product, rich in meat, and a simple advertising phrase which expressed its quality, the words *"Lean Red Meat"* spelled out in big red letters. Our agency adopted this

Nothing
satisfies
the inner dog
like
lean red meat*

Ken-L Ration

packed with lean red meat
...steaks, chops and roasts of
*U.S. Govt. Inspected Horse Meat
and other healthful nutrients.

successful line and put it next to a picture of the meat. That was all that was needed to send out an atavistic signal to the reader concerning acceptability and good nutrition.

The anthropomorphic aspects of the dog were expressed in cartoons that showed various types of dog personalities, while avoiding the wagging tails and lolling tongues so common in other dog food advertising.

Ken-L Ration continued in first place for several years.

Sometimes it is better to compress a proposition that is complex psychologically, into simple symbolic terms.

The most pervasive theme in gasoline advertising over the years has been power. The most durable symbol of power has been the tiger, currently used by Exxon in various parts of the world. The slogan "Put a Tiger in Your Tank" was developed by our agency in 1959 for the Oklahoma Oil Company, a chain of stations in Chicago that had just been purchased by the Standard Oil Company of New Jersey (now Exxon). The advertising shown here marked the birth of this long-lived animal.

Put a tiger in your tank!

OKLAHOMA ANNOUNCES A FABULOUS NEW GASOLINE:

HIGH-Q EXTRA WITH HP!

Now! A completely new Super Premium Gasoline . . . the greatest gasoline sold in this area! HP Compound in new HIGH-Q EXTRA actually brings back the power and pep your car had when it was new! You get more power because HP drastically cuts down misfiring caused by short-circuited spark plugs. You get smoother performance because HP controls the pre-ignition that makes cylinders fire at the wrong time. And you get better gasoline mileage because HP reduces gasoline waste resulting from misfiring and pre-ignition. Put this Tiger in your tank today! Start your car on a new life with Oklahoma's sensational new HIGH-Q EXTRA — enjoy "Happy Motoring" . . . once again!

OKLAHOMA

Valuable prize coupons, too!

Le Car Hot

LEÇON FRANCAISE DE L'AUTOMOBILE *or,* *how to make your driving fun again.* **L'ÉCONOMIE:** get up to 40 mpg; go on a week-end trip on one tankful of gas; use the savings to buy things you've been putting off! Le Confort: 4 doors for easy-out, easy-in; astounding head-room, foot-room; fatigue-free riding. LA MANEUVRABILITÉ: scoot in, around, through and out of heavy traffic easily; turn effortlessly; only 155 inches (!) of car to park. Le Dealer Network: over 800 coast-to-coast sales, service and parts headquarters, 150 more in Canada. *La BEAUTÉ: styled in Paris, made in France; six solid colors to choose from,* handsome contrasting upholstery. LES EXTRAS: very sporty sliding sun-roof, Ferlac automatic clutch, both optional. LA GRANDE DIFFÉRENCE: EVERYTHING YOU WANT IN A CAR (INCLUDING A 7 CU. FT. TRUNK) AND YET ONLY $1645.*POE N.Y. *Le Next Step?* See *your nearest Renault Dealer for a test drive. You'll be pleasantly surprised at how much fun is waiting for you – HONEST!*

Le Car Hot: **RENAULT** Dauphine

SUGGESTED RETAIL PRICE, FEDERAL AND LOCAL TAXES EXTRA. FOR ILLUSTRATED BROCHURE SEE YOUR LOCAL DEALER OR WRITE: RENAULT, INC., 750 THIRD AVENUE, NEW YORK 22, N.Y. ALSO ON OVERSEAS DELIVERY PLAN.

In 1958, this campaign began for the Renault Dauphine. The car was introduced into a market dominated by increasingly bigger and "finnier" American cars. An import in those days was a curiosity. Gasoline prices were so low that mileage was not an issue. The main reason for buying a Dauphine, apart from its low sticker price, was the fact that it was French. This advertising made its origin unmistakable and helped launch it on a successful career, ended only when Volkswagen invaded and took over the import market.

Continental Airlines

Good airline advertising makes it clear where the airline will take you, in what degree of comfort, and for what price. The best of it also communicates something called "character." In airline advertising, "character" combines all the factors that suggest things are going to work right. Courtesy, neatness, and punctuality all contribute to this feeling of confidence.

Discover the Continental States of America

Lots of countries form their own airlines. But as far as we know, this is the first time an airline has formed its own country.

Continental did... to show you where our Proud Birds go, and more important, to show you how we are different.

Our difference is pride. Continental's people take an almost patriotic pride in their airline. You can feel it... in all the little,

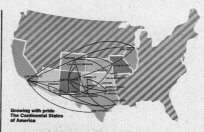

Growing with pride
The Continental States
of America

extra things they do for you. Like helping you choose the best fare for your budget, double checking your reservations, making sure your meal is properly served. The result is that you have a real feeling of comfort and confidence.

In the C.S.A., come travel with us and feel the difference pride makes. Your travel agent or Continental will arrange it. Please call. If you're a "foreigner," you may never be satisfied with your own airline again.

Continental Airlines
the proud bird with the golden tail

The bigger and better known the airline, the less it should have to talk about these things. In an era of extraordinary safety records and standardized training, it doesn't pay to say too much about what the customers already expect. The sheer style of the advertising can often express this part of the message better.

If you are a smaller regional airline, competing on the same routes against the majors, things are different. You have to lay out your credentials. When our agency got the Continental Airline account in 1965, this airline already had a devoted following, won by exceptional attention to this matter of "character."

Continental opens its "NW/SE territories"

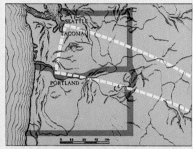

Wouldn't you know it! The Continental States of America is only a few months old and we're experiencing our first territorial expansion.

A recent route award has made it possible for us to add the states of Washington, Oregon and Louisiana to the C.S.A. This means the present number of states in our country

stands at twelve, instead of the previous nine ...and we're very excited about that.

But the real story is even bigger. For the first time, the Pacific Northwest and the Gulf Coast have a direct jet connection...no more plane changing. Continental Airlines now provides service between Seattle / Tacoma, Portland, Wichita, Tulsa, Oklahoma City Houston and New Orleans.

This means a new opportunity for more people to travel more places in the Continental States of America and feel the difference pride makes.

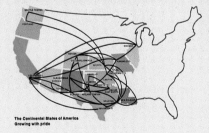

The Continental States of America
Growing with pride

Continental Airlines
the proud bird with the golden tail

However, not enough travelers knew where the airline went, or what unusual attention it paid to service amenities.

To communicate both these things, the agency created *"the Continental States of America,"* a simple and dramatic way of showing routes. The "citizens" of this "country" were, of course, the employees, who took great pride in good service. *"Feel the difference pride makes,"*

1

Most countries are real

2

like the United States of America, including Alaska and Hawaii, of course. But there's a new country that isn't really real.

5

On Continental Airlines the difference is pride, the almost patriotic pride of Continental's people.

6

They do everything in an exacting thoroughness that makes you feel good, comfortable, confident.

became the slogan of the airline. It served the airline well as the route structure and staff expanded. It was used internally to sustain already high morale; and it was heavily merchandised in flight.

Deregulation has now shifted the emphasis in airline advertising to price, but this campaign still stands as an example of how airline "character" can be expressed without frozen grins, sunset landing shots, or other clichés.

3

We call it the Continental States of America. Continental Airlines invented it to show you where our proud birds go and, much more important, to help you remember how we're different.

4

Since all airlines use the same kind of planes, all have terminal facilities, and most offer you a choice of coffee, tea, or milk, what is the difference?

7

In the Continental States of America, come travel with us and feel the difference pride makes. Continental Airlines.

8

Proud bird with a golden tail.

THE MANY FACES OF FOOD ADVERTISING

Our agency has been fortunate in having three long-time food clients; Kraft (since 1934), The Campbell Soup Company (since 1954), and General Mills (since 1962). Each of these companies has a remarkable record of moving, over the years, from a narrow product base (cheese, flour, soup) to a widely diversified line of foods. This has been done with the help of advertising (from a number of agencies) which has allowed the companies to direct carefully orchestrated appeals to a more and more diverse and segmented market.

Food, along with automobiles, is one of the most widely advertised categories in the USA. At any given time, about 2,000 food items are being advertised in general media (not counting retail price advertising). Much of this advertising goes unnoticed; it is just too inert. However, food advertising is not confusing or wasteful as some observers say it is.

People *buy* food for survival; but they *shop* for a wide range of values. They bring to shopping remarkably clear ideas of what they want and what it is worth. Advertising helps them sort out their options in advance. People look at food advertising with the same canny sense of values. They reject nonsense and vacuity, and go straight for the brand that presents them with clear-cut values.

What makes the creation of food advertising so challenging is that the basic scenario of eating is so familiar and repetitive: the food is prepared; it is looked at; it is eaten; there are reactions, vocal, gestural, or visceral. Then it is time to wash the dishes.

Efforts to liven up this homey scenario with borrowed interest (geographical, sociological, theatrical) very often fall flat. Where food is concerned, it is dangerous to get too far from fundamentals. However, there is plenty to work with. In addition to appetite appeal, there is a whole complex of values associated with cooking, eating, and diet. Food can be an expression of caring, hospitality, and status. It can reflect health concerns all the way from specific medical problems to just plain belly filling. In advertising, almost any kind of food responds to good art direction.

The trick is to use only the appeals appropriate to the product, and then to use them with just the right restraint or abandon.

Some examples of our work in this vein follow.

General Mills

The advertisements for three General Mills products on this and the following pages look nothing alike. Each reflects the character and function of the product. To be effective, food advertising has to show great sensitivity to where the product fits into changing meal patterns, and into the purchaser's scheme of things.

1980: Hamburger Helper is as close to being a sheer utility product as any food product can be. It does not respond to ornate presentations.

This animated hand expresses exactly what the product does, in a tone that reflects its function.

1962: This Betty Crocker Mix advertisement
was run when a new flavor was still news. The
formal layout suggests the ceremonial uses of
the product. The endorsement of General
Mills' corporate doyenne, Betty Crocker, is
prominent.

1985: Cake and other desserts are still
symbolic of love and hospitality. But this
current advertising reflects more casual meal
habits. Copy in a lighter vein has taken over
from the more deliberate statements of an
authority figure.

Betty Crocker is the leading brand of dessert
mixes.

And you thought Bisquick only made pancakes.

Impossible Zucchini-Tomato Pie

The pie that does the impossible by making its own crust.

2 cups chopped zucchini	1½ cups milk
1 cup chopped tomato	¾ cup Bisquick baking mix
½ cup chopped onion	3 eggs
½ cup grated Parmesan cheese	½ teaspoon salt
	¼ teaspoon pepper

Heat oven to 400°. Grease 10-inch quiche dish or pie plate, 10 x 1½ inches. Sprinkle zucchini, tomato, onion and cheese in plate. Beat remaining ingredients until smooth, 15 seconds in blender on high or 1 minute with hand beater. Pour into plate. Bake until knife inserted in center comes out clean, about 30 minutes. Cool 5 minutes. 6 servings.

High Altitude: Bake about 40 minutes.

Join the Bisquick Recipe Club. See package for details. Send $3.00 to General Mills, Inc., Box 5183, Minneapolis, MN 55460.

® Bisquick is a registered trademark of General Mills, Inc. © General Mills, Inc. 1982

1981: Bisquick is the leading all-purpose baking mix, stocked in over half of all American houses. As its traditional uses decline, new uses have to be promoted. It is shown here as an ingredient for a very contemporary main dish.

In recipe advertising it is better to be simple and straightforward. Readers look for only two things: the end result, and how to get it.

Kraft's Parkay Overcomes Boredom

Every so often, the advertising for the leading brands in a category begins to look just as much alike as the products do. Claims and images overlap and cancel each other out. People become confused and begin to yawn at the advertising or, worse yet, to laugh at it. Advertising dollars begin to lose their value. When advertising for a category becomes thus ridden with clichés, it is time for the daring to strike. That is what Kraft did with Parkay Margarine.

In 1973, Kraft's Parkay Margarine was a poor second in its market and its share of the market had been sliding. Two years later, Parkay was in a solid number one position. What happened?

Then, as now, the shopper peered into the dairy case at five or six heavily advertised brands of margarine. Choosing her brand was not a big decision and she would quickly move on to other purchases that had much greater impact on the family diet and budget. All she was really looking for was something she knew mixed and spread easily, and tasted pretty much like butter.

Competing brands used advertising that came as close as possible to suggesting that their brands not only tasted like but *were* butter.

Research showed that Parkay did indeed have a better taste than most of its competitors. The trick was to find a way to say "It tastes like butter" in a unique and involving way.

The answer was the "talking cup" campaign featuring a surprising and funny dialogue between the box and a skeptical customer. An unforgettable product personality was created before the viewer's eyes. It was clearly nobody else's commercial.

Eleven years later the campaign was still running and still working. Its credibility and success were measured regularly and still held up. Parkay sales continued at a peak.

1

Cup: Butter.
Vic: What was that?
Cup: Butter.

2

Vic: Parkay Margarine.
Cup: Butter.

3

Vic: No, Parkay—it says right on your lid, Parkay Margarine.
Cup: Butter.
Vic: Parkay.

4

Vic: Mmmmmmm, smooth, delicious! Butter!

5

Cup: Parkay.
Vic: Oh, you.

6

Parkay Margarine. From Kraft. The flavor says butter.

The Loud, Commanding Voice of V-8 Vegetable Juice

There is no such thing as an "established" product. There are only products moving along the trajectories of their life cycles. A product's life can be prolonged and enhanced with the right advertising. Sensing when a product is reaching its peak, and then reintroducing it with excitement and surprise, is often the key to its survival. With a mature product, this requires busting loose from all previous advertising forms.

A few years ago, sales of Campbell's V-8 vegetable juice hit a plateau. Enough people knew about V-8 and liked it to have greatly increased its sales *if* they had bothered to use it. The real clue to its problem was that an alarmingly high percentage of its admirers had tucked a can or two way back in their cupboards and forgotten about it. V-8 was all dressed up, but people hadn't asked it to the party.

Year after year, a fact-laden print campaign had told people how good it was for them. Like an aging ingenue, the more its healthy qualities were proclaimed, the duller it got.

Then, Campbell broke the pattern. All of a sudden, over 20,000,000 radios, a strange sound was heard. A voice that could shatter glass proclaimed *"Wow, it sure doesn't taste like tomato juice! It's got a taste all its own! Great!"* The medium (radio) was new for V-8. The sound was unprecedented, and the message gave the main reason for its acceptance in the first place—its flavor, quite distinct from tomato juice, its main competitor.

People paid attention. (They had to.) Sales began to increase. Over the first five years that this theme was used (with adaptations to keep it fresh) sales continued to rise at an average of about 9 percent a year.

By timely restaging and surprise, V-8 had been moved from the back of the customer's mind to the front; and from the back of the cupboard onto the table.

BRAND CHANGING: RISKY BUSINESS

How Arco Changed Three Brands into One and Came Out Ahead

When the brand of a product or service is changed, it seldom benefits anybody except the advertiser. It can be a risky business strategy. People buy by brands. Brands are repositories of trust, good will, and value perceptions. A poorly communicated brand change can lose all these elements of brand personality, and lose the marketer his business. Arco did it right.

In 1970 and 1971, the Atlantic Richfield Corporation carried out one of the biggest brand changes of all times. The company had acquired 24,000 service stations under three brands, Atlantic, Richfield, and Sinclair. All three brands were strongly entrenched in their respective regions. In spite of this, it was decided to create a new nationwide identity. *All* stations would be changed to the Arco brand. Station façades and facilities would be upgraded, and new, improved gasolines would be introduced. All of this was to be accomplished in twelve months.

Early test results, in which signs were simply switched from Atlantic and Sinclair to Arco, showed the risk involved. Without customer preparation by advertising, gallonage in test stations dropped up to 20 percent, wiping out their profit margins.

The agency's research confirmed that casual highway customers were skipping the new sign, and driving on to gas stations with long-established brands. It seemed that, even though most drivers believed all gasolines were alike, there were still factors of trust and familiarity that won out when the driver had a choice.

The advertising strategy therefore almost wrote itself: convince the driver that nothing had changed, that the new steel sign, standing coldly in the wind, still stands for value and friendly service.

This, however, could be a rather ponderous message. The agency reduced it to its simplest possible terms with humor and humanity. It treated the change pretty much like a thorough spring cleanup. A massive media schedule made this less-than-worldshaking event visible to almost 90 percent of Arco's customer groups. The copy played the event down, while the media plan played it up.

The campaign proved that it was possible to transfer loyalty to a new brand, if the event was presented simply, visibly, and with suitable modesty. Within a year, the new brand had achieved a recognition factor of 80 percent. More important, the company had maintained its overall market share and had actually gained in some areas, producing a 6 percent increase in gallonage rather than the 20 percent decrease suffered in the unadvertised test markets.

1

Dino: Ya know Ed, you guys are doing pretty well now.
Ed: Yep.
Dino: You changed all your Sinclair Stations.
Ed: Yep.
Dino: To Arco Stations. Yep, you've got new Arco Supreme, our gasoline that helps your car breathe easy.
Ed: What are you driving at?

2

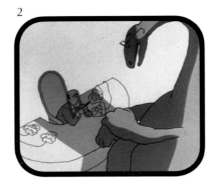

Dino: Look, I've had my eye on a great little swamp just outside Miami. What I really want to do is go down there and take it easy for a couple a'hundred years.

3

Dino: Just mess around in the mud and get to know myself a little better.

4

Dino: Well ya know Ed, you don't really need me anymore.
Ed: Now, now wait a minute...
Dino: No Ed, I think a guy should know when to quit.
Ed: Quit, —Well you just...
Dino: Uh ha, I got some money saved up; stock, profit sharing.
Ed: Well if it's money you'll be needing—
Dino: No, no. What I'm trying to tell ya is, 37 years is enough for anybody.

5

Atlantic Richfield announces the end of the dinosaur era.

6

We're sad to see him go, but with the end of one era is the beginning of another.

The Arco Circle

It's 200 miles North of the Arctic Circle. It's 300 miles from the nearest city. 6 months ago, it rented for 900 million dollars.

It's the North Slope of Alaska. It's the place Atlantic Richfield Company, manufacturers of ARCO brand petroleum products, found, at Prudhoe Bay, the first major oil field on American soil in 40 years.

In doing so, we turned one of the most desolate, forbidding places on the face of the earth into one of the most sought after places on the face of the earth.

Major oil companies paid nearly 900 million dollars to the state of Alaska for leases.

Now suddenly all of Alaska has a bright new future. And the oil find will provide numerous jobs in areas that had no other kind of work before, other than hunting and fishing.

Atlantic Richfield is the company behind your local Richfield service station.

We went all the way to Alaska so your local Richfield dealer can continue to give you better products for your car. In that way, the Arco Circle covers the whole country.

This advertisement was part of the campaign that helped establish a new corporate personality for the Atlantic Richfield Company. During a time of acute oil shortages, it dramatized Arco's pioneering role and enormous investment in the new Alaskan oil fields.

The Sinclair dinosaur, one of America's best known gasoline trademarks, was phased out with this commercial. Other commercials appropriately phased out the Atlantic and Richfield brands.

73

Honda Makes It Simple

A car buyer has to be comfortable with the statement, "This car is me." This state of comfort occurs after he is exposed to all kinds of evidence: how the car looks; what other owners say; who the other owners are; how the dealer treats him; how the car drives; what it costs; and what the advertising says.

Unlike some simpler products, a car's brand personality cannot be created by advertising alone. But advertising can confirm what the prospect sees and hears on the street and it can get him into the showroom. It can also amplify his feelings about the car's "fit." Is it a "good set of wheels," a symbol of affluence, a projectile, or a muted expression of good taste?

For car advertising to work, it has to be true to what the car really represents in terms of hard values and the perception of its best prospects. Where the car-maker has a clear-cut, people-oriented philosophy, this too can be a valuable ingredient of the advertising.

That has always been the case with Honda.

In 1973, Honda introduced its small Civic automobile into a turbulent U.S. market. Due to the oil crisis, small cars were gaining in favor. Detroit seemed unable to produce an acceptable small car. Volkswagen, which had had the market to itself, was declining. But Toyota and Datsun were coming on strong with rapidly expanding lines. The import market was cluttered with at least 15 makes.

Honda's philosophy, born of a single-minded pursuit of engineering excellence, said "keep it simple."

In this expanding world of new import models, styles, and options, Honda focused on economy and value. Refinements of style and a wide range of models would have to wait.

This was the right strategy for a market that was refocusing from power and prestige to more basic values. By 1976, Honda's relentless engineers had produced a Civic with the best gas mileage of any automobile sold in the United States; and in 1976, its first generation Accord combined both performance and styling. Honda was noticed; first by the buffs, then by a growing segment of the new practical-minded prospects.

Honda was rapidly reaching that critical mass of perceptions that adds up to a brand personality. Buyers were saying "Smart Buy;"

74

The Honda Civic. The car we designed around a shopping bag.

It's true. We had supermarket shopping bags flown to our factory when we designed the Honda Civic® Hatchbacks. Measuring the bags helped us determine the size of the rear cargo area.

This may seem like a lot of fuss over a small detail. But at Honda we do everything that way. For all its simplicity, the Honda Civic has been planned with meticulous care.

So you see? It's not by accident that four full-sized shopping bags fit inside our hatch.

Of course, four also happens to be the number of full-sized people that fit inside our Civic's passenger compartment. And if we went to all that trouble to make a shopping bag comfortable, just imagine what we must have done to make you comfortable.

HONDA
We make it simple.

© 1978 American Honda Motor Co., Inc. Civic® is a Honda trademark.

Why we make it simple.

Honda set out to design one car that suited the basic transportation needs of the entire world.

So to help us discover that basic design we studied and analyzed data from 91 different countries. We collected information on everything from road conditions in Morocco to rainfall in Denmark to the dimensions of the average motorist in the United States.

In time the answer became clear. If Honda was to fill a universal need, we would have to build a simple car.

Simple to drive, simple to park, simple to understand, simple to own.

Today we offer three simple cars. The Honda Civic 1200, the Honda Civic CVCC; and the Honda Accord.

Consider for a moment how simplicity can help minimize just one of today's many automotive problems: the cost of gasoline.

All Hondas meet emissions requirements without a catalytic converter. So all Hondas run on regular as well as unleaded gasoline.

But don't be misled. A simple design is often the most difficult. For all their simplicity, Hondas are among the most sophisticated cars in their price range.

There is, of course, another reason why we make simple cars. The reason is you. We know that choosing a new car can be a complex problem.

It's a problem, however, that we can solve quite easily by giving you your choice of just three cars.

There. Now haven't we made your life simple?

HONDA
We make it simple.

HONDA CIVIC CVCC SEDAN   © 1978 American Honda Motor Co., Inc.   *Civic 1200 not available in California. Civic®, CVCC®, Accord®, and Civic 1200 are Honda trademarks.

"Best in its Field;" "What you give up in space you get in performance;" "Not bad looking, either."

During this same period, the advertising expressed Honda's philosophy and the values it offered.

In 1977, the first major campaign broke in magazines and TV. The theme was *We make it simple.* The layouts were clean and uncluttered and so were the commercials. Everything projected an image of simplicity and solid value. This advertising was true to the product, and true to the way people were apt to perceive it. It reinforced all the good impressions people had of Honda, and then added to them. It made virtues out of the short line, the limited color choice, and (at first) the limited options. It said, in effect, "we understand you really want basics, so we focused on those instead of the frills."

Our engine sits sideways so you don't have to.

When people sit in a Honda Civic* 1200* or Civic CVCC* for the first time, they are often surprised at the amount of room inside.

They discover that despite their brief overall length our Civics have plenty of room for four adults. Plus luggage space behind the rear seat.

How do we do it? To help solve the mystery, we took the roof and hood off a Honda Civic CVCC Hatchback.

As you can now see, one reason for the Civic's roominess is the way the engine sits. Because it sits sideways, instead of

lengthwise, the engine doesn't interfere with front-seat legroom. Instead, it is neatly tucked away up front, out of everybody's way.

Of course, the engine in our Civic CVCC 4-speed Hatchback is sitting pretty when it comes to fuel economy. This model got 42 mpg for highway driving, 36 mpg city, according to EPA estimates. The actual mileage you get will vary depending on the type of driving you do, your driving habits, your car's condition and optional equipment. Mileage estimates are lower for California and high altitude cars.

Getting back to roominess. We gave the Civic additional space by giving it front-wheel drive. This means there is no drive-shaft to the rear wheels, so the hump running through the passenger compartment is reduced.

So now when you sit in a Honda Civic, please don't be surprised that you're not cramped for space. And that you're not sitting sideways.

After all, it was a simple matter to make our engine sit that way instead.

HONDA
We make it simple.

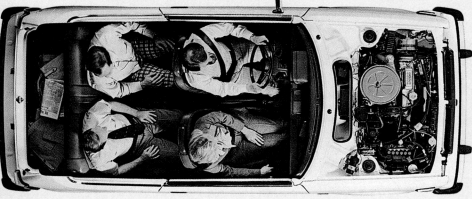

HONDA CIVIC CVCC 4-SPEED HATCHBACK.

This campaign continued into the launching of the advanced 1982 model Accord, one of the most successful cars in automotive history. This clear, understated approach continues today with a much broader line of Hondas, including the performance-oriented Prelude.

The car-buying public was apparently ready for simple propositions, simply presented. Honda ranked 23rd out of 25 among all import nameplates in 1970. By the end of 1984, it had moved into second place and was pressing Toyota for first.

Honda's success is a victory of the "Honda Way" as expressed through product, perceptions, and advertised personality. It also reflects, not only the high quality of Honda dealers, but Honda's special relationship with them, characterized by full, open, and straightforward communications.

The Big Honda.

There is big, and there is big. So you may not think the Honda Accord is a big car. After all, it's only 162.8 inches long. And that's a good deal shorter than the Chevrolet Monza's 178.6 inches.

But the outside dimensions of a car don't always tell you how big it is inside. And that's where the Accord may surprise you.

Like all Hondas, the Accord has a transverse-mounted engine with front-wheel drive. This means the engine is tucked away up front, out of the way, and there is no drive shaft to the rear wheels. The space we save by this configuration is turned over to our passengers in the form of roominess and comfort.

With the rear seat folded down, the Accord converts to a roomy cargo carrier. Its hatchback design permits easy access to the fully-carpeted rear deck. And a lever by the driver's seat lets you release the hatch before you get out of the car.

Regardless of its size, the 1978 Honda Accord is definitely big on standard features. Its base sticker price includes an AM/FM radio, automatic maintenance reminder and electronic warning system, tachometer, steel-belted radial tires, rear window wiper, washer, and defroster, and

our CVCC° engine, which runs on regular or unleaded gasoline.

Having mentioned gasoline, we should tell you that the Accord is big on mileage, too. With its standard 5-speed transmission it got 44 mpg for highway driving, 33 mpg city, according to EPA estimates. Of course, the actual mileage you get will vary depending on the type of driving you do, your driving habits, your car's condition and optional equipment. Mileage estimates are lower for California and high altitude cars.

Right here we would like to reassure you on one point. Although we fondly refer to the Accord as the Big Honda, it is only big by our standards. We don't build what are traditionally called big cars. And we don't intend to start.

A big car wouldn't be as simple to park as the Accord. Or as simple to maneuver in city traffic. And if we can't make it simple, we don't make it.

HONDA
We make it simple.

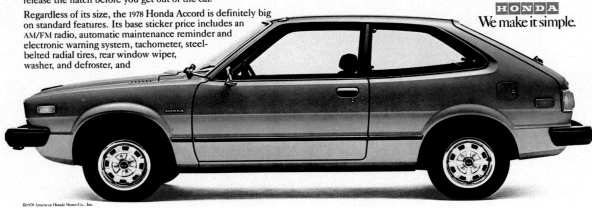

©1978 American Honda Motor Co., Inc.

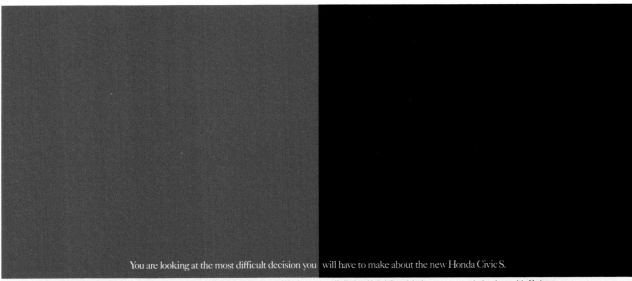

You are looking at the most difficult decision you will have to make about the new Honda Civic S.

The Civic 1500 S Hatchback is so special it's painted special colors. Red or black.

The red Civic S comes equipped with performance features. Just like the black.

The black Civic S drives like a sports car, yet remains a Honda. Just like the red.

Both cars have identical S type suspensions. For less suspense through the curves.

© 1982 American Honda Motor Co., Inc.

This new system includes front and rear stabilizer bars, sport shock absorbers and Michelin steel-belted radials.

By lowering the final drive ratio, we increased the acceleration. We coupled our responsive 1488cc overhead cam engine with our smooth-shifting 5-speed transmission. The S is quick.

The brakes match its performance. And the ventilated front discs and rear drum brakes are power-assisted and

self-adjusting with dual-diagonal circuits.

The Civic S looks fast even standing still. Notice the blackout exterior trim. The accented side moulding. And the air dam up front.

Halogen headlights come standard. And so do the dual remote-controlled side mirrors.

The interior for both cars is basic black with red seat inserts. And the front seats are comfortable contoured

buckets that you sit in. Not just on.

Your hands fall comfortably on the sporty four-spoke steering wheel. While your eyes fall on the tachometer and quartz digital clock.

The rear window wiper/washer helps keep your rear vision clear. That's important.

When you look at everything, choosing the Civic S is easy. *Which* Civic S is difficult.

HONDA
We make it simple.

This is a 1979 Honda Civic.

We've sealed and supported the inside and filled it to the top of the window with water.

Now we're pumping it into this car.

The new 1980 Honda Civic. It has a longer wheel base, an improved suspension for a smoother ride, and 20% more window area for better visibility. All this without adding an inch to the overall length.

The 1980 Honda Civic is completely restyled this year from the simplified front end and longer profile...

to the enlarged hatch for easier loading. And now the best part. We've gotten over 13% more space on the inside; that means more room for your legs, your shoulders...

or your goldfish.

Honda—We make it simple.

79

Advertising the New Passenger Train Service

In 1975, the agency went to work for Amtrak. At that time, passenger train service was showing the effects of 20 years of neglect. Much of the equipment, roadbeds, and stations were run down and out of shape. Employee morale was low.

Over that same 20 years, the nation's airlines had matured into the major mass carrier, and the new Interstate Highway system had made auto and bus travel easier than ever. What was the place of the passenger train?

Amtrak's federal subsidy is based on the premise that a fuel-efficient alternative to air and highway travel is important to the nation's economy and security. Furthermore, there was an important base of service to maintain. In spite of all the problems, over 16-million passengers still rode the trains each year. But for the system to be economic, ridership had to increase dramatically.

The reconstruction of the nation's passenger train service is a story of great management skill and dedication that will be told in full some day. One measure is that by the end of 1984, train ridership had risen from 17.4 million (in 1975) to 19.9 million or 14 percent. This was a direct result of the exhaustive reequipment, rebuilding, and retraining that had gone on, and the right advertising. The passenger train had been restored to a degree of acceptance that many skeptics had thought impossible.

Advertising can only proclaim what has already been accomplished. Over nine years our work for Amtrak evolved with the system itself. Great care was taken never to overstate what various parts of the system could offer. For these reasons, most Amtrak advertising was on a route-by-route basis.

In 1977, the national slogan was *"We've been working on the railroad,"* a somewhat tentative statement. In 1980, as work progressed in the system, the line was changed to *"America's Getting into Training."* In 1983, it was possible to change again to a more positive and challenging slogan, "All Aboard Amtrak!"

Perhaps the most striking example of what reconstruction and advertising together could accomplish was the Metroliner Express Service between New York and Washington. This is the most crowded travel corridor in the country. About 17,500 people a day travel by railroad alone. By 1981, crowded airplanes and heavy auto traffic had seriously affected public attitudes towards these carriers. That year,

Amtrak finished its track improvements and new equipment was ready. Travel time had been cut to just under 3 hours from downtown to downtown versus 2½ hours by taxi and plane.

The new Metroliner Express Service was announced quite simply, but with great media impact— "New York to Washington in 2 hours and 59 civilized minutes." (Today it takes "2 hours and *49* civilized minutes.")

The result was immediate and dramatic. Ridership on the new trains reached an all-time high for the system. On the run as a whole, ridership went up an average of 15 percent a month for the first three months, and continues to grow.

The advantages of train travel on this route are obvious to anyone who has tried it. It is true that on other routes, the longer the trip, the more value the traveler has to place on ambiance. The results of this campaign show that the quiet, stress-free quality of train travel, although once almost forgotten, can again become highly valued.

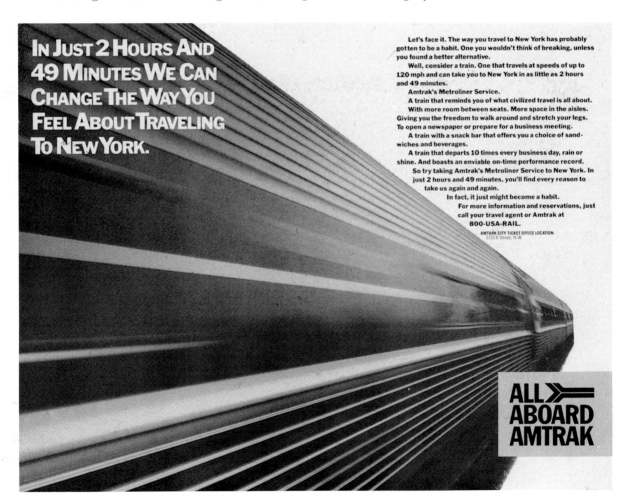

IN JUST 2 HOURS AND 49 MINUTES WE CAN CHANGE THE WAY YOU FEEL ABOUT TRAVELING TO NEW YORK.

Let's face it. The way you travel to New York has probably gotten to be a habit. One you wouldn't think of breaking, unless you found a better alternative.

Well, consider a train. One that travels at speeds of up to 120 mph and can take you to New York in as little as 2 hours and 49 minutes.

Amtrak's Metroliner Service.

A train that reminds you of what civilized travel is all about.

With more room between seats. More space in the aisles. Giving you the freedom to walk around and stretch your legs. To open a newspaper or prepare for a business meeting.

A train with a snack bar that offers you a choice of sandwiches and beverages.

A train that departs 10 times every business day, rain or shine. And boasts an enviable on-time performance record.

So try taking Amtrak's Metroliner Service to New York. In just 2 hours and 49 minutes, you'll find every reason to take us again and again.

In fact, it just might become a habit.

For more information and reservations, just call your travel agent or Amtrak at 800-USA-RAIL.

AMTRAK CITY TICKET OFFICE LOCATION:
1721 K Street, N.W.

ALL▶ ABOARD AMTRAK

2 Hours And 49 Civilized Minutes To Washington.

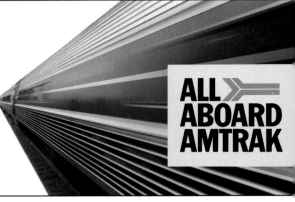

ALL ABOARD AMTRAK

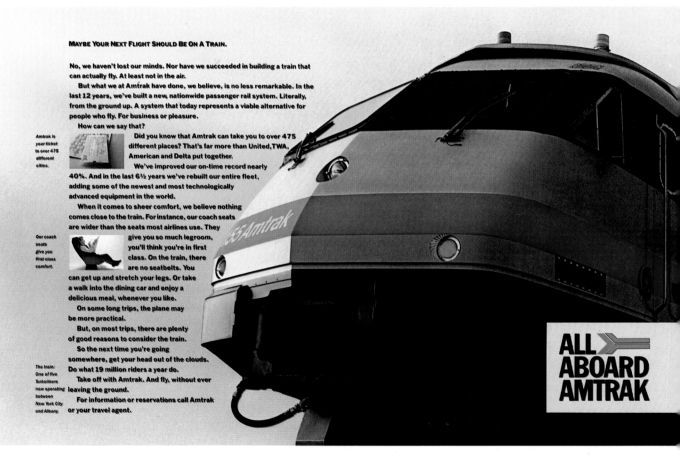

MAYBE YOUR NEXT FLIGHT SHOULD BE ON A TRAIN.

No, we haven't lost our minds. Nor have we succeeded in building a train that can actually fly. At least not in the air.

But what we at Amtrak have done, we believe, is no less remarkable. In the last 12 years, we've built a new, nationwide passenger rail system. Literally, from the ground up. A system that today represents a viable alternative for people who fly. For business or pleasure.

How can we say that?

Amtrak is your ticket to over 475 different cities.

Did you know that Amtrak can take you to over 475 different places? That's far more than United, TWA, American and Delta put together.

We've improved our on-time record nearly 40%. And in the last 6½ years we've rebuilt our entire fleet, adding some of the newest and most technologically advanced equipment in the world.

When it comes to sheer comfort, we believe nothing comes close to the train. For instance, our coach seats are wider than the seats most airlines use. They

Our coach seats give you first class comfort.

give you so much legroom, you'll think you're in first class. On the train, there are no seatbelts. You can get up and stretch your legs. Or take a walk into the dining car and enjoy a delicious meal, whenever you like.

On some long trips, the plane may be more practical.

But, on most trips, there are plenty of good reasons to consider the train.

So the next time you're going somewhere, get your head out of the clouds.

The train: One of five Turboliners now operating between New York City and Albany.

Do what 19 million riders a year do.

Take off with Amtrak. And fly, without ever leaving the ground.

For information or reservations call Amtrak or your travel agent.

ALL ABOARD AMTRAK

Xerox and the Office of the Future

Business machines are complex forms of hardware, sold in an extremely complex marketplace. For many years, these products could be advertised pretty much as hardware, but during the seventies, the variety and sophistication of business machines increased enormously. So did the number of people who bought and used them. Copiers, duplicators, printers, word processors, small computers, and data transmission systems completely changed the work environment—and came to have a broader and broader effect on office efficiency and morale at all levels. They became, in fact, a real part of daily life for millions of people.

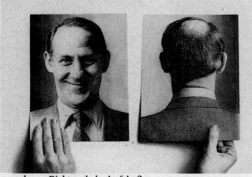

As new products appeared, Xerox continued to present them with clarity and warmth. This consistency helped build sales and acceptance for the corporation.

1973

The new machines could help, but they could also hinder. The more complex the system, the more havoc was caused by breakdowns and service delays. The reputation of the manufacturer, therefore, became as important as the immediate benefit of the machine.

Over the same period, the audiences for business machine advertising became wider and wider, as more people used them and had a say in their purchase. Virtually all of white-collar America could be considered at least marginally influential in shaping the market.

For all these reasons, it was no longer enough to advertise "hardware." Competitive capabilities were equalizing. In the new environment, what the manufacturer was really selling was less drudgery, greater speed of operation, reliability, and accuracy. The end benefits were greater productivity and greater work rewards.

From the start, the Xerox Corporation anticipated the rapidly changing needs and atmosphere of its markets.

1979

Xerox is ready to admit everything isn't all black and white.

We at Xerox have known as well as anyone that skies aren't always gray.

But until now, there wasn't anything even we could do about it.

Naturally, we were working on the problem. And now our work has paid off. Brilliantly.

The Xerox 6500 <u>color</u> copier is here. ///
In all its glory.

It gives you copies as sharp and clear as you'd expect copies made on any of our machines to be.

With one little exception: they're in vivid color. Like the rest of the world.

This ad was originally conceived in black and white. But you have to admit, you might not have read all this if we hadn't used color.

In fact, we've used color in this ad in some of the ways we think you should use it in your business. To communicate. To attract attention. To make a point.

Now that the news about our new color copier is out, we're sure that many companies will be delighted. Of course, there are a couple who just may turn green.

XEROX

Xerox. The duplicating, computer systems, telecommunications, education, micrographics, color copier company.
And to think you knew us when.

1973

1980

Xerox introduces the Information Outlet.

If you're wondering how business will handle information in the '80s, the handwriting is clearly on the wall.

We call it the Information Outlet—a new way for you to custom design an information management system that will give you maximum flexibility with minimum expense.

Here's how it works:
The Information Outlet gives you access to a special Xerox Ethernet cable that can link a variety of office machines. Including information processors like the Xerox 860, various electronic printers and files, and, of course, computers.

The Xerox Ethernet network will

enable people throughout your company to create, store, retrieve, print and send information to other people in other places—instantaneously.

This network wasn't designed to work exclusively with our equipment. Other companies' products can be connected as well.

As your needs change, so can your network. You'll simply plug in new machines as you need

them—or as technology develops better ones.

So, through the Xerox Information Outlet, you'll get to the future the way the future itself will get here.

One step at a time.

XEROX

If you'd like more information on the Information Outlet, write us and we'll send you a booklet: Xerox Corporation, P.O. Box 470065, Dallas, Texas 75247.

The rise of Xerox began with its 914 copier, introduced in 1959. By 1968, when our agency got the account, Xerox was already one of the fastest growing of Fortune 500's leading corporations. It had clearly filled a gaping hole in office technology. Refinements and extensions of the basic xerographic process continued to pour out of the Xerox laboratories.

The business machine category was still one of relatively low interest, and competitive advertising had a print shop flavor to it.

The Xerox 9200 copier/ duplicator was launched in 1975 with this award-winning commercial. The 9200 was a key addition to the line designed to compete with offset machines and to move Xerox into a much broader up-scale market. It was also a statement of Xerox's growing high tech capabilities. The commercial focuses clearly on the product benefit in a context that is both unique and winning. Brother Dominick became one of Xerox's best salesmen.

1

Anncr: Ever since people started recording information,

2

there's been a need to duplicate it.

6

Stephens: Brother Dominick, what can I do for you?
Monk: Could you do a big job for me?

7

Anncr: Xerox has developed an amazing machine that's unlike anything we've ever made—the Xerox 9200 Duplicating System. It automatically feeds and cycles originals...has a computerized programmer that coordinates the entire system.

86

Fortunately, Xerox management was already committed to advertising styles that set the company apart.

From the start, our agency used a combination of fact and subtle humor. Wherever possible, demonstrations were used, but technical detail was left to the salesman and the spec sheet. The advertising focused on a single key benefit, presented clearly, but with disarming warmth. Every communication of Xerox had to project not only technical proficiency, but a sense that Xerox understood office management problems and the people who had to deal with them.

3

Very nice work, Brother Dominick.
Brother: Thank you.

4

Now, I'd like 500 more sets!

5

(muttering away) 500 more sets?

8

Can duplicate, reduce and assemble a virtually limitless number of complete sets. And does it all at the incredible rate of two pages per second.

9

Brother: Here are your sets, Father.
Father: What?
Brother: The 500 sets you asked for.

10

Father: It's a miracle.

In the late '70s, the electronic typewriter began to transform the secretary's work style, replacing the older electrics. The Xerox Memorywriter appeared in 1981 and leapfrogged all other products in its field; it offered greater speed and innovative word processing capability. It was introduced with advertisements like the one below, which tell simply and dramatically why it is superior. Within three years, it achieved leadership, which it shares with IBM in this new and dynamic market.

Our new typewriter has more memory than what's their name's.

You know who we mean.

The one that sells the most typewriters.

The fact is, our new typewriters simply outclass theirs.

You see, not only can secretaries use the Xerox 610 Memorywriter just like the simple electric they're used to. But it also comes with a memory that saves them an incredible amount of time and trouble.

It handles margins, tabs, column alignment, indents, centering and underlining with unbelievable ease.

And can automatically erase what's been typed. Not just character by character, but entire lines at a single touch.

It lets you use three different type sizes and proportional spacing. All on one machine.

And the 610 Memorywriter remembers about 30% more characters than you-know-who's comparably priced model.

That's 30% more addresses, dates, names, phrases or entire paragraphs that your secretary doesn't have to keep retyping.

What's more, with any of the Xerox Memorywriters, you'll be able to add as much memory as you need. As you need it. Without changing machines.

So when you need a new typewriter, don't settle for an ordinary electric.

Especially when you can get your hands on a Xerox Memorywriter.

The typewriter that'll make you forget everyone else's.

For information, call 800-648-5888, operator 269, your local Xerox office, or mail in the coupon below.

☐ Please have a sales representative contact me.
☐ I'd like to see a demonstration.
☐ Please send me information about your new Memorywriters.
Mail to: Xerox Corporation, Box 24, Rochester, N.Y. 14601.

Name_____ Title_____

Company_____

Address_____ City_____

State_____ Zip_____ Phone_____

In Nevada, call 800-992-5711, operator 269.

XEROX

XEROX® and 610 are trademarks of XEROX CORPORATION.

88

She lived through slavery.
The Civil War.
The Civil Rights Movement.
She lived to be 110.
Yet she never lived at all.

Tonight Cicely Tyson stars in The Xerox Season presentation,
"The Autobiography of Miss Jane Pittman." 9 P.M. Eastern Time. CBS-TV.

XEROX

From the beginning, Xerox management has had a deep sense of social
responsibility. This has been expressed with flair and impact in many ways, not the
least of which has been through television programming.

"The Autobiography of Miss Jane Pittman," sponsored by Xerox in 1974, is one
of the most honored TV specials of all time. It was part of a twenty-year record
during which Xerox brought exceptional, and often controversial, programs to the
air. Shows like Alistair Cooke's "America," Bill Cosby's "Of Black America,"
and "Generations Apart," were part of a continuing commitment to associate the
corporation with better television programming.

EATING OUT: FROM PIT-STOP TO TREAT

Advertising and the McDonald's Image

For most Americans, thirty years ago, eating out had one common denominator: *unpredictability.* You didn't know how you'd be treated by the help, you didn't know how the fellow guests would behave, and you didn't know how the food would taste, or how clean the kitchen was. All these uncertainties and fears come to a head at the old-time fast food restaurant. On the road, it was often little better than a pit-stop.

Then along came Ray Kroc. He learned his business firsthand and he saw the problems that needed solving. He brought *predictability* to a business with widely varying standards. That meant that the customers' expectations of quality, cleanliness, quick service, and a reasonable price were *always* met at *any* McDonald's: no exceptions.

Kroc started out with one drive-in; that was hard enough. As the chain grew, he evolved methods of quality control, building design, maintenance, employee training, and franchise motivation that worked, no matter how many stores were involved. The "Hamburger Stand" was no more. It became a store, and then it became a restaurant, with a longer and longer menu. The uniform values still held up. You could see the kitchen and it was clean. There was no hassle with a fickle staff. The total transaction was reduced to its bare essentials. The food was uniformly good; so was the atmosphere. McDonald's was not a hangout; it became more and more the family restaurant.

The management genius that brought this about continues today and is reflected in more than 8,500 stores worldwide. In a mobile world, a fundamental need had been met.

When our agency began work for McDonald's in 1970, the fast food industry still had a dingy image as a result of its past practices. The McDonald's formula was working, and the company was gaining fast on the leading chain, Kentucky Fried Chicken. However, too many people still thought of eating fast food as a last resort.

The agency's job was to break through these negative perceptions all at once. What emerged was the campaign, *"You deserve a break today...so get up and get away to McDonald's."* The advertising changed the language of fast food advertising. It established a new framework that embraced all the values McDonald's offered—the total experience. It got people thinking in terms of McDonald's as a special place to go, a family treat, and a place to seek relief from daily pressures.

Commercials were meticulously cast to show the kind of people McDonald's sought to attract. As all good service advertising should, it showed employees behaving the way McDonald's wanted them to. The advertising thus reinforced the real-life impressions of how both other customers and servers looked and acted.

The words and music worked hand in hand with these very human visual images. The theme, *"You deserve a break today,"* was used steadily for five years and intermittently thereafter. The song, at the height of its exposure, reached the unprecedented level of 80 percent recognition by the general public. Research showed that the commercials not only delivered the message, but were genuinely liked by a vast majority of respondents.

In the face of competition, the advertising was changed in 1974 to further personalize it. The new theme, *"You, you're the one ... we do it all for you,"* allowed the advertising to focus better on individual items in the rapidly expanding menu. It did so without sacrificing the warm, real-life situations that had set new standards everywhere for narrative of television commercials.

Our agency created the national advertising for McDonald's for eleven years. During that time McDonald's achieved dominant leadership in its field. This was against growing competition that had learned to apply some, if not all, of Ray Kroc's operational concepts.

Over those eleven years, McDonald's annual sales volume grew from $550 million to over $6 billion. It expanded successfully overseas from Germany and the U.K. to virtually the entire Pacific Basin. Everywhere, its operational standards were kept intact, and appropriate variations of U.S. advertising were used.

The McDonald's story is a classic example of management innovation, genuine consumer value, and advertising that projected the resulting benefits in a totally new and convincing way.

Cleaning Up

1

Grab a bucket and mop. Scrub the bottom and top. There is nothin' so clean as my burger machine.

2

With a broom and a brush. Clean it up for the rush. Before you open the door.

3

Put a shine on the floor. When we're finished, what then? Start all over again!

4

Tell me what does it mean? At McDonald's it's clean.

5

You deserve a break today …

6

So get up and get away to McDonald's. McDonald's.

92

Establishing the Theme

1

So much life to be lived, So much to be tried

2

and with the sharing you get

3

—a special feeling inside, it's a full-time thing, the kind of life that you lead.

4

A little break from it all is the break that you need.

5

You deserve a break today. So get up

6

—and get away...to McDonald's.

7

You deserve a break today.

8

So get up and get away

9

To McDonald's.

Introducing Breakfasts

1

*Nobody rises up in the morning
quite the way we do*

2

the crack of dawn, hot coffee's on

6

You're the reason we do it.

7

Nobody can do it

3

a glorious day breaking for you.

4

Those stirring sounds, those crisp hash browns.

5

Say it's morning, hope you'll drop in.

8

like McDonald's can.

9

10

95

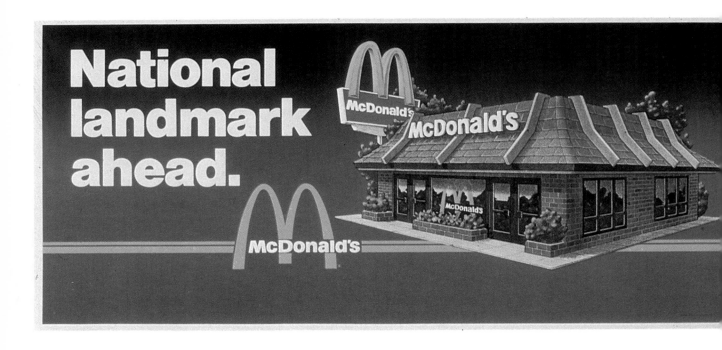

ADVERTISING TO CHILDREN—A SPECIAL RESPONSIBILITY

Companies who advertise to children take on a special responsibility. These companies cannot be expected to alter social values, but neither should they degrade them by using images of violence (which are already too prevalent in programming), or by reinforcing ethnic or sex stereotypes.

Children must never be disappointed by advertising. Their sensitive responses to authority and showmanship have to be understood, so that, whatever the product is, they get what they are promised.

The creative problem is to use fantasy and/or contemporary images of fun, without distorting values or in any way stretching the truth.

McDonald's Ronald

Ronald McDonald was not invented by our agency, but his turf and retinue were expanded by us, with many new and wonderful creatures.

Ronald, himself, is the ultimate clown, spreading innocent joy with which children can identify. His young followers have told our research people that they get what he promises at McDonald's.

Campbell's SpaghettiOs

"Mr. O" is a puppet who looks roughly like a
SpaghettiO, one of Campbell Soup's most popular
products. He presides over lively little vignettes which
tell what SpaghettiOs are and why they are fun to eat,
without stretching any points.

General Mills' Fruit Bars

Better look out, Mama,
Look out Dad,

It's the ugliest

goody I ever had.
New Fruit Bars.

So good and ugly.

The commercial for General Mills' nutritional "Fruit Bars" describes them as "good and ugly," an expression that effectively translates into fun and good taste.

Wrigley's Hubba Bubba

BIG BUBBLES, NO TROUBLES.

Wrigley's "Gumfighter" has been captivating audiences for over five years. In a mawkish takeoff on old Western movies he shows why Hubba Bubba bubble gum offers "Big Bubbles, No Troubles." The product is a best seller.

Anheuser-Busch Builds Brand Personalities

The concept of product personality is probably more important in beer advertising than in any other category. Beer is a social drink. Beer drinking is an experience rich with associations. In many ways, beer comes to represent the environment in which it is consumed. It also represents what the beer drinker wants that environment to be. Good beer advertising relates a brand to the best of these associations.

The quality and price of a brand of beer set the rough boundaries of its market. It is up to the advertising to flesh out the personality of the brand so it appeals to as much of its potential market as possible.

The success of Anheuser-Busch is due to many things, primary among them extraordinary attention to quality. It is also due to skillful orchestration of a number of brand personalities aimed at different kinds of beer drinkers.

Our agency started to work on Busch Beer in 1977. This was followed by our assignment to Bud Light in 1981 and Michelob Light in 1984. Each of these brands is evolving a distinct and quite different brand personality as shown in the following three examples.

Busch Beer

Advertising for Busch Beer, a medium-priced brand, has a rugged, honest, straightforward tone. Although it uses familiar Western imagery, it does so with words and pictures of unusual impact and credibility. The slogan "Head for the Mountains" fits its market. The brand is gaining share in markets where it is being promoted.

Michelob Light

*Advertising for Michelob Light addresses the young,
up-scale market for this higher-priced light beer. The
images catch the lifestyle of the urban, upwardly
mobile beer drinker.*

Bud Light

Suppose that's them.
Don't know who else'd be out this early.

For the Caldwells, early morning's the best time to get things done. And times being what they are, not much would make them shut down.

Even for a few minutes.

But this summer of 1984 the Caldwells have shut down to see something they'll most likely never see again.

As we host the games this summer, let's hope we all learn the true meaning of the Olympics is not in the winning. But in discovering the best in all of us.

This commercial for Bud Light Beer was produced for the 1984 Olympics, of which Anheuser–Busch was a sponsor. It evokes the spirit of the Olympics in simple, moving terms. It shows how an advertiser can be visibly supportive of events like this with both relevance and taste.

How Sears Stays Young

There are very few great corporations that can match the continuing capacity for self-renewal of Sears, Roebuck and Co.

Back in 1925, the company dramatically changed its thrust from catalogue merchandising to retail store operations. This put Sears in a position to attract millions of people who, for the first time, were finding it easy to drive to town to shop.

In the '50s and '60s, as the cities spread outwards, Sears also moved out from the central city. Its innovative store designs came to dominate many of the new suburban shopping centers.

During the same period, the amount of advertising for products competitive to Sears was growing fast. Brand consciousness was increasing. People were buying by brand in categories that, before, had been regarded as staples.

Sears responded by developing its own brands, characterized by solid values at reasonable prices. No retailer had ever succeeded in doing this on such a broad range of products.

In the '70s and '80s, with the growth of the major discounters, Sears began to encounter stiff competition in price. As for quality, Sears was pressed by the growth of boutique and specialty merchandisers. Sears' answer is yet another form of self-renewal. It is a new kind of store and a new style of merchandising designed to meet the challenges of the discounter, the specialty retailer, and nationally advertised brands.

Sears' new "Store of the Future" remains a department store, offering Sears' full line of merchandise and services. However, it avoids the austerity of the price merchandisers on the one hand, and the random, messy quality of the boutiques on the other. The new Sears' store gives its customers a sense of discovery. The displays are colorful, but also logical and disciplined. Shoppers can find what they want quickly and on their own. The wide variety of choice projects value without bargain basement atmosphere.

An integral part of the program is national advertising. To dramatize the new look, our agency developed the line, *"You're in for a change at Sears."* As the new policies took hold, the line became, *"There's more for your life at Sears,"* which is now used on all lines of merchandise.

The Goolagong line of sports-oriented clothing is presented with fast-paced visuals and music.

1

2

3

4

1

2

Advertising for the Open-Home line of home furnishings has a more conservative flavor and deliberate pace.

3

4

Our agency also does the advertising for the clothing and home furnishings lines, much of which were also redesigned. In these volatile areas, a careful balance has to be kept between contemporary and traditional designs in order to span the wide range of tastes represented by the 39 million households served by Sears. The same balance applies to the advertising.

In television, the retail advertiser does not have the luxury of time to present the goods in great detail. A lot of information on quality, styling, and price must be conveyed in a few seconds. Too often, this leads retailers to use frantic, overstylized scenarios that have high visibility but convey little information. The keys are to be selective, and to use a style consistent with the product.

The commercials shown here for Goolagong and Open-Home are complete, without being congested. Their respective styles are consistent both with the product values, and with Sears' overall personality. These two lines are among Sears most successful introductions.

As with all good retail advertising, it is hard to tell where the advertising ends and the store begins.

Lands' End Direct Merchants

Direct Response Advertising is the fastest growing sector of American merchandising. For twenty years, Lands' End Inc. has been selling an expanding line of unpretentious but extremely well-made merchandise. For the last five years, our agency has done the advertising for Lands' End. The copy and art style have an earthy, plain-spoken quality that matches the goods. These three advertisements for a briefcase, shirts, and their guarantee typify the effort that has helped make Lands' End one of the fastest growing of all direct response merchandisers.

Three of the best pulling ads from the Lands' End campaign.

The world is full of guarantees, no two alike. As a rule, the more words they contain, the more their protection is limited. The Lands' End guarantee has always been an unconditional one. It reads:

> *"If you are not completely satisfied with any item you buy from us, at any time during your use of it, return it and we will refund your full purchase price."*

We mean every word of it. Whatever. Whenever. Always. But to make sure this is perfectly clear, we've decided to simplify it further.

GUARANTEED. PERIOD.

LANDS' END
DIRECT MERCHANTS
of fine wool and cotton sweaters, Oxford button-down shirts, traditional dress clothing, snow wear, deck wear, original Lands' End soft luggage and a multitude of other quality goods from around the world.

☐ Please send free catalog.
Lands' End   Dept. J-09
Dodgeville, WI 53533

Name
Address
City
State _____ Zip

Or call Toll-free:
800-356-4444
(Except Alaska and Hawaii call 608-935-2788)

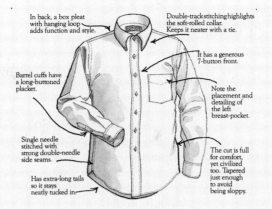

In back, a box pleat with hanging loop adds function and style.

Double-track stitching highlights the soft-rolled collar. Keeps it neater with a tie.

It has a generous 7-button front.

Barrel cuffs have a long-buttoned placket.

Note the placement and detailing of the left breast-pocket.

Single needle stitched with strong double-needle side seams.

The cut is full for comfort, yet civilized too. Tapered just enough to avoid being sloppy.

Has extra-long tails so it stays neatly tucked in.

We set out to make the world's best buttondown. This one comes close. At $25.

This is the Hyde Park—the latest addition to our impressive Oxford Collection, featuring both shirts of 100% cotton and our Lands' End reverse cotton blends.

Check it out feature for feature, beginning with the knowledge that it's made of imported 100% cotton Oxford. Heavier. More densely woven for a nicer drape. It launders better, resists wrinkles; best of all, it wears longer than normal.

For those of you interested in more specifics, we've provided this step-by-step "tour" of the shirt—available in pink, ecru, blue, maize, helio and white solids, as well as stripes and tattersalls, too.

Why make so much of a single shirt? We may have told you more than you ever wanted to know about a shirt. But only to make a point about the Lands' End philosophy of doing business.

It is a simple philosophy really:

First, quality. Then, price. And always, always service.

A quality item at a reasonable price represents a Lands' End value. Anything less is someone else's ballgame—not ours. What's more, every item we offer you—from soft luggage to sweaters to snow wear to shoes—is unconditionally guaranteed.

We don't ask you to trust us, just try us. Mail the coupon for a free catalog. Better still call our toll-free 800 number. 800-356-4444. 24 hours a day (except Alaska and Hawaii call 608-935-2788).

☐ Please send free catalog.
Lands' End   Dept. J-09
Dodgeville, WI 53595

Name
Address
City
State   Zip

LANDS' END
DIRECT MERCHANTS
of fine wool and cotton sweaters, Oxford button-down shirts, traditional dress clothing, snow wear, deck wear, original Lands' End soft luggage and a multitude of other quality goods from around the world.

Or call Toll-free:
800-356-4444
(Except Alaska and Hawaii call 608-935-2788)

Why this New York ad man leaves his $300 attaché case in the closet and carries our $39.50 Square Rigger.

Dick Anderson, an Executive Vice President of Needham, Harper and Steers, explains it this way:

"I'm always trying to jam more things into an attaché than it was ever meant to hold. That plays hell with stiff-backed cases. So I find myself leaving my $300 leather case in the closet, and carrying my canvas Square Rigger. It swallows overloads without complaint, has inside pockets for my calculator and appointment book, even a snap hook for keys."

And more.

That's not even the whole story of our Square Rigger. It's made of tough yet soft 18 oz. Square Rigger cotton canvas. Has comfortable padded handles. Smooth-operating YKK zippers. Comes in six businesslike colors.

Pretty impressive for $39.50. And we'll add your monogram for just $5 more.

We make the Square Rigger and over a hundred other Lands' End items at our duffle works in Boscobel, Wisconsin. That way we can guarantee the best possible materials and workmanship. And sell our soft luggage to you without middleman mark-ups.

First quality, then price.

What we have to offer goes beyond soft luggage, even beyond our great sportswear and accessories. The Lands' End tradition affects everything we offer you.

First, quality. Then, price. And always, always service.

That's why we offer a guarantee that would put lesser merchants out of business. Simply: "If you are not completely satisfied with any item you buy from us, at any time during your use of it, return it and we will refund your full purchase price."

If we're new to you, we don't ask that you trust us. Just try us. By phone, you can reach us toll-free 24 hours a day at 800-356-4444 (except Alaska and Hawaii call 608-935-2788). Or fill in the coupon. Order a Square Rigger or not, as you like. But let us send you a free copy of our Lands' End catalog.

☐ Please send free catalog.
Lands' End   Dept. J-09
Dodgeville, WI 53595

Ship____ Attachés $39.50 ea.
plus $2.50 shpg. ☐ Tan ☐ Navy ☐ Green
                  ☐ Brown ☐ Grey ☐ Burgundy

$5.00 to monogram 3 initials ☐ ☐ ☐

☐ Check enclosed   ☐ American Express
☐ Visa   ☐ Master Card

Card No.
Expiration Date
Name
Address
City
State   Zip

LANDS' END
DIRECT MERCHANTS
of fine wool and cotton sweaters, Oxford buttondown shirts, traditional dress clothing, snow wear, deck wear, original Lands' End soft luggage and a multitude of other quality goods from around the world.

Or call Toll-free:
800-356-4444
(Except Alaska and Hawaii call 608-935-2788)

How ITT Set the Record Straight

Gossip loves a vacuum. When people do not understand what a major institution does, they make up stories about it. The bad ones usually stick. The bigger and more influential the corporation, the more important it is that people understand what it does and what it stands for. The best way to express this is in terms of what its real social value is—what *it* does for people—*in very specific terms.*

In 1972, ITT was the fastest growing multinational conglomerate in the world. It was doing business through over 200 companies in most of the free world. It is not surprising that few people had a clear impression of what ITT produced or what social purpose it served.

1

2

I'm not an actress—I'm a school teacher and I'm going blind. A disease called Retinitis Pigmentosa is taking my sight away. I can still see by day. But in the dark, when you're still able to see things, the

world to me looks like this.

5

6

But when it is, there'll be some pretty grateful people.

To you, this may seem ugly.

To add to this problem of perception, the early seventies was a period of strong antibusiness feeling. This was aggravated both in the U.S. and abroad by strong political crosscurrents.

In this atmosphere, it became vital that ITT, the most visible multinational conglomerate, be better understood for what it was. The perception needed to be changed from that of an enigmatic social force to that of a responsible business force yielding clear-cut social benefits—as well as a good return to its shareholders.

In developing corporate advertising, the temptation often is to wrap the company in the flag—or to drape it with benign generalities. This tends to leave a company's image as fuzzy as ever, and its credibility no better and possibly worse.

With ITT, there was no room for this kind of cheerful but empty practice. Instead, it was agreed to explore ITT's vast and growing

3

There's a device that can help me. You're looking through one

4

just like the one I have. With this, I can see in the dark again. ITT developed it, and they're working now with the Retinitis Pigmentosa Foundation to help tens of thousands of people like me. They're working on a less expensive, pocket-sized model. It's not available yet.

7

To me, it's beautiful.

8

ITT. The best ideas are the ideas that help people.

technological resources to find specific and dramatic examples of ITT's contributions to the common good.

The agency found this surprisingly easy. ITT was on the leading edge in communications technology, and in wide areas of medical, nutritional, agricultural, and transportation technology, among many others.

The agency began filming a series of 60-second "documentaries" dramatizing specific ITT products in use all over the world. The theme of the campaign was *"The best ideas are ideas that help people"*—a theme that was never used without concrete support.

This campaign ran for twelve years.* Annual tracking studies showed a doubling of "awareness and familiarity" with ITT in just three years. Since then, the public perception of ITT has continued to improve.

A dangerous information vacuum was filled, and a major corporation's reputation greatly enhanced. Facts, dramatically presented, continue to be the key.

---

*Since 1984 an account of Biederman & Co.

RCA: One of a Kind

In 1984, we were asked by RCA to develop a corporate advertising program. Under its remarkable chairman, Thorton Bradshaw, the company had redirected and revitalized itself over a three-year period. But its great and growing strengths in communications, electronics, and entertainment were very unevenly recognized by the financial community and the public. It was, in fact, the only company with leadership positions in all three of these fields. The theme, *"RCA: One of a Kind,"* positions the company as unique. The art and copy present startling and specific examples of the company's achievements. This is another example of the importance of clear-cut communications goals in a field full of fuzzy generalities.

WHY RCA IS ONE OF A KIND.

In the vast universe of corporations, RCA stands alone. Certainly, others manufacture television sets. Still others are major forces in communications, broadcasting, defense and aerospace. But no other company does all of the things that RCA does.

That distinction not only makes RCA unique, it has enabled us to develop talents and abilities that, we believe, no other single corporation possesses.

Three years ago, new top management at RCA took a long, hard look at those talents and abilities. And at the industries in which we compete. The resulting strategy was a simple one – do what we do best. In short, focus on three businesses that offer the greatest potential for future growth – electronics, communications and entertainment.

The results have been dramatic. In home video systems RCA has built a leading market share in television receivers, video cassette recorders and cameras. And we're pioneering the ingenious charge-coupled-device (CCD) in a revolutionary broadcast camera that can practically see in the dark.

In space, our business has taken off. RCA is the leader in the design and construction of both communications and meteorological satellites. And our cameras and video equipment are playing a major role in the Space Shuttle program.

AEGIS, the Navy's seaborne weapons defense system, was developed and built by RCA. The first two cruisers in this new series are now in service and we've been awarded contracts for eleven additional ships.

In 1983, NBC captured more prime-time Emmy Awards than the other two networks combined. RCA Records had a smash year with hits by Kenny Rogers, Alabama and Hall & Oates. And, in conjunction with Columbia Pictures, RCA has become a leader in prerecorded music/video cassettes.

This tremendous success has had another effect – RCA's earnings in the second quarter were the highest in the Company's history.

If these facts surprise you, write to us at: This Is RCA, P.O. Box 91404, Indianapolis, Ind. 46291 and we'll send you a few more surprises. You see, we want you to rethink RCA. As a corporation, as an investment or as a place to work. Because when you do, you'll realize that RCA really is one of a kind.

RCA
ONE
OF
A KIND

113

This 1962 billboard for Mars is addressed to candy eaters of all ages.

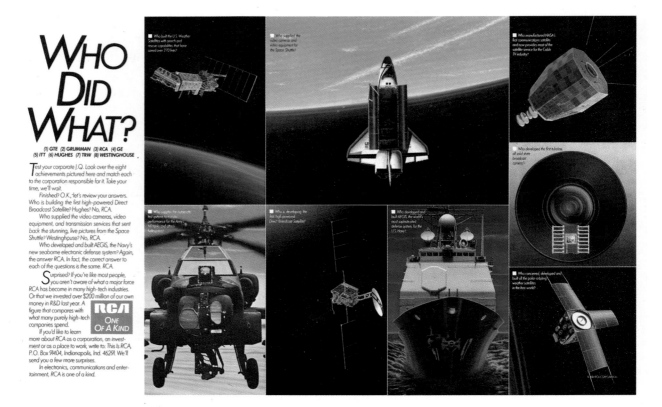

This 1984 ad for RCA is addressed to broad segments of the business community.

The Milky Way billboard aims to sell 25¢ candy bars.

The RCA advertisement aims to revitalize the image of a great corporation.

The Milky Way board dramatizes the familiar. The RCA advertisement dramatizes the unfamiliar.

Although the RCA ad presents more data, both ads are remarkably simple projections of the values each one represents.

Like the rest of the work in this book, they both adhere to the creative guidelines spelled out in the front of this book:

1. They *establish clear-cut personalities* for what is being advertised.
2. They *position their subjects clearly.* (You eat one; you invest in the other.)
3. They *feature the most compelling benefit* (the pleasure of little witches; strength in growth industries).
4. They *break the pattern* of advertising in their respective categories.
5. They *generate trust* (with Milky Way, let us call it "the willing suspension of disbelief").
6. They *appeal to both heart and head.* (Although the RCA advertisement solicits a cool-headed response, it also projects the excitement of discovery.)

The markets that these advertisements address seem far apart, but their common audience, as for all advertising, is the listening, looking human being, willing to learn, and willing to buy, if the proposition is presented with skill and care.

Keeping Going

As I write these concluding words, I find myself rejecting the word "postscript." It has a terminal quality that doesn't fit a book that is a kind of midterm report. As I write, at least a dozen of our creative teams are working on campaigns that will certainly shake up their respective markets. The streets and the bush are full of new songs and species. The best half of the story is yet to be told.

It has been widely noted that our industry is in convulsive change. It may well be. However, I believe that good ideas and good people will survive. Let the industry conform to them. If it doesn't, it will broach and founder.

This is a business in which theory runs thin. It is a tactile, hands-on kind of business. Good ideas come only after rubbing up against the grain and the grit of the marketplace. Then, illuminations tend to come in a rush; on a train ride, at night, in a canoe. The process is dynamic and not precise.

The right idea comes first. Then comes the transaction. The best client-agency relationships have a give-and-take quality in which the authorship of the idea can be forgotten and nobody cares. These transactions are also dynamic and are often imprecise.

Life in advertising often seems like a compressed series of defeats and victories. Victory is better, but defeat need not be devastating. When a client says "no" with finality, it may be a professional defeat, but if the agency's position is well prepared, and stoutly defended, it is not a moral defeat.

In a purely professional issue, it is possible to lose with honor. In a moral issue, where integrity or self-respect are involved, it is not. In many ways, the test of a true professional is being able to distinguish a professional issue from a moral issue.

My partners over the years, whose pictures adorn the following pages, are true professionals. Jim Isham, Blair Vedder, the late Bill Steers, and Keith Reinhard all worked with me in the series of transitions that marked the growth of the agency. Each brought something special to the business.

Jim Isham brought a keen sense of creative values and a cool and balanced judgment that never wavered.

Blair Vedder brought business sense raised to the highest level of intelligence. He gave us a hearty style of management that was at once considerate and realistic.

Bill Steers was a man of inimitable charm and showed great insight into the personal aspects of our business.

Keith Reinhard is the blazing talent behind much of the later work in this book. He now brings the same force and originality to other agency operations, along with a capacity for firm and sensible management.

An advertising agency is really nothing more than a confederation of people who agree to work together to make the most of their talents. The only contract between us is an unwritten bond made up of common standards, mutual respect, and good will.

When the right people get together in this spirit, as they have at our agency over the years, you get motion, you get fire, and you get great advertising.

James Isham

*President of Needham, Harper and Steers from 1967 to
1976, the year he retired. He joined the agency in
1948.*

1962: Paul Harper and Jim Isham receive the agency's first assignment from General Mills from its president, General E.W. Rawlings. This marked a breakthrough for the agency's new management team.

Blair Vedder

*President of Needham, Harper & Steers from 1976 to
1980; Chairman of the Executive Committee and Chief
Operating Officer from 1980 to 1982; Chairman of
Needham, Harper & Steers International from 1982
until his retirement in 1984. He joined the agency in
1948.*

122

1970: Blair Vedder working the territory. Shortly after he helped the agency acquire the McDonald's account, Blair Vedder enrolled in Hamburger University, Oakbrook, Illinois, the McDonald's training school.

William Steers

Chairman of the Board of Doherty, Clifford, Steers and Shenfield, until its merger with Needham, Louis and Brorby in 1965. Chairman of the Board of Needham, Harper & Steers from 1965 to 1967. Chairman of the Policy Committee from 1967 until his retirement in 1969.

Paul Harper

President and Chief Executive Officer of Needham,
Louis and Brorby (later Needham, Harper & Steers)
from 1964 to 1967. Chairman of the Board and Chief
Executive Officer from 1967 until his retirement in
1984. At present, Chairman Emeritus. He joined the
agency in 1946.

Keith Reinhard

President, Needham, Harper & Steers, Chicago, from 1980 to 1982. Chairman and Chief Executive Officer of Needham, Harper & Steers, U.S.A. from 1982 to 1984. Elected Chairman of the Board and Chief Executive Officer of Needham Harper Worldwide, Inc. in October, 1984. He joined the agency in 1964.

September 14, 1984: Paul Harper, retiring Chairman, congratulating Keith Reinhard on his election as the new Chairman and Chief Executive Officer of Needham Harper Worldwide, Inc.